D1328445

A Christian's
Handbook on
Communism

The Greater Hartford Council Of Churches
835 Pearl Street   Room 204
Hartford 4, Connecticut

A
Christian's
Handbook
on
Communism

 **Committee on World Literacy
and Christian Literature**

First Edition   1952

Second Edition   1955

Third Edition
Revised and
Enlarged   1962

Published for
The Committee on World Literacy and Christian Literature
of the
NATIONAL COUNCIL OF THE CHURCHES OF CHRIST IN THE U.S.A.
by the
Office of Publication and Distribution
475 Riverside Drive, New York 27, New York

Copyright ©, 1962 by Committee on World Literacy and
Christian Literature

D 01-54 $1.00   Printed in U.S.A.

Foreword

The first edition of *A Christian's Handbook on Communism* grew out of four months of intensive study by a group of Christian workers from many countries. In this study the group collected and discussed the main facts about communism that confront Christians today. The essence of their findings was put into form for publication by a group of Latin American workers. Christian leaders around the world used this booklet in study and action seminars, and as one result of this study at least twelve other books on the same subject, in as many languages, were published to alert churches abroad to immediate dangers that communism poses.

This revised and enlarged edition updates the description of Communist theory and practice and outlines the nature of the Christian faith and its expression through the church. In this objective study, the facts speak for themselves on an issue that cannot be resolved by emotional response. Leaders in church circles, educational institutions, and government have given counsel, information, and fresh insights during the preparation of this edition.

This document is not an official publication of the National Council of the Churches of Christ in the United States of America. It is a statement prepared for and approved by the Committee on World Literacy and Christian Literature of the Division of Foreign Missions of the Council. The Executive Board

[v]

of this Division took the following action with respect to it on February 2, 1962:

> "VOTED: That the Executive Board commends *"A Christian's Handbook on Communism"* to the General Board of the National Council of the Churches of Christ, to member boards and agencies of the Division of Foreign Missions, and to literature committees of Christian Councils overseas for prayerful study and for such purposeful action as they may deem wise."

Dr. Eugene Carson Blake, Chairman of the General Public Interpretation Committee of the Council, in his report to the General Board on March 2, 1962, said:

> "The Committee encourages the widespread use of this Handbook by the churches as the basis for intelligent analysis and discussion of the doctrines of Communism viewed from the perspective of Jesus Christ."

The General Secretary of the Council, Dr. Roy G. Ross, in his annual report to the General Board expressed the hope that it would be commended by the leaders of our member denominations to their local congregations.

All Bible quotations in this book are from the Revised Standard Version, copyrighted 1946 and 1952 by the Division of Christian Education of the National Council of the Churches of Christ in the United States of America. Credits for other quoted material will be found on pages 85 and 86.

Contents

Chapter 1 | The Power and Appeal of Communism

Roberto, remembered as one of the best students who ever attended a certain Christian school in Brazil, had never known a real home. The teachers in the Colegio soon seemed like parents to him, and their friendship transformed his whole life. He began to attend church. He became active in the young people's society and was soon elected president. Later he joined the church and for a time served with great enthusiasm as superintendent of the Sunday school.

Then Roberto went to the university. A few months later he stopped attending church. One of his teachers tried several times to visit him but never found him home. Letters to Roberto brought no reply.

After several months Roberto appeared one night at his former teacher's office. During their conversation the student said, "I don't believe all these superstitions any more. I'm a Communist now. Christians only talk about changing the world; the Communists are the ones who are really doing it. They are solving our problems and offering us a better life. From now on just count me out as far as the church is concerned."

Before Roberto left he told the teacher that he had been expelled from the university but that he did not really care. Now he was living for a great cause!

That conversation opened one teacher's eyes. He realized as never before that communism has power because it provides the oppressed people of the world with a program for change that Roberto had not found in Christianity. Roberto's teacher saw clearly that the struggle of this century is a struggle for the souls of men.

The Christian's life has always been one of struggle. Jesus found himself faced with opposition throughout his earthly ministry. His enemies nailed him to a cross. His followers in every country across the centuries have had to wrestle "against the principalities, against the powers, against the world rulers of this present darkness. . . . " (Ephesians 6:12). These forces have often been hidden in the ordinary temptations of every day. From time to time, however, they have appeared in the guise of overwhelming social or political movements, such as the Roman demand for emperor worship, which tested the faith of early Christians, and Nazism, which challenged the Christian church more recently. Today Christians are confronted with communism, one of the most powerful mass movements of the Christian era, a movement that rules over one-third of the world's population and has adherents and agents around the globe.

Why has this happened? What is the appeal of communism to Roberto and millions of other people like him? What are the main points of its attraction? To answer such questions it is necessary to look thoughtfully at the plight of the peoples of the world and the promises that communism makes to give them hope.

Every day the majority of the world's people face poverty, hunger, unemployment, disease. They are victims of illiteracy, exploitation, political corruption, discrimination, and oppression. They long for respect and freedom, for food, good homes, health, education, and employment with adequate pay. At present, however, they see no sure way of life at all, no future for themselves or their children. Many are confused and without purpose. Any voice that offers them a way out of their difficulties will be heard, and communism is such a voice. It attracts both the hopeless and the social idealist because it offers clearly a philosophy, a passion, and a plan of action—the same elements of mind, heart, and strength with which dedicated Christians present and express the Christian faith.

A Philosophy

Communists says that communism is the philosophy of hope and faith in humanity. They believe that man possesses the abil-

[2]

ity to control his destiny. They are convinced that mankind is advancing out of darkness toward a life in which war, poverty, and misery will be unknown. This belief gives communism its strength.

For many persons in the mechanical, industrialized world of today, life has lost all meaning. To them communism offers a philosophy that seems to explain the world and to promise to make their own individual lives count for something in the march of human history. It claims to know the secret of a "scientific" method for setting this world right. Such persons have stated that it was only through their contact with communism that life began to make any sense or to have any purpose.

A Passion

It is not difficult to see how appealing such ideas are and why many people have been led by them to adopt this apparently optimistic philosophy. But communism offers more than a philosophy of life. It provides a passion, a strong, emotional drive that demands the complete devotion of its followers. A young Russian who gave himself to communism shortly after the revolution in that country described the dramatic power of that new system as follows:

> The newspapers were shrill with the call to a better life for the country. Poor and backward Russia was at last on the highroad to progress—it only remained for everyone to dig more coal, raise more grain, acquire more culture. I read the invocations as if they were addressed personally to me. . . . I felt myself part of something new, big, exciting. . . . Now life had for me an urgency, a purpose, a new and thrilling dimension of dedication to a cause. I was one of the elite, chosen by history to lead my country and the whole world out of darkness into the Socialist light. . . . There were defects, extensive suffering. But there was also the life of terrific excitement and inflamed hopes. . . . To people like myself, possessed by the idea and the faith, today's pain seemed only a necessary payment for the glorious future awaiting the country and its people.[1]

The author of these words has long since renounced communism, but it is easy to see where its original appeal lay for him. Drawn largely by emotional pulls, he joined a great movement; he gained a sense of power and achievement; and he discovered a new faith that roused him to a religious type of fervor and devotion.

Another dedicated Communist expressed her feelings about communism to a traveler from the West in these convincing words:

> We have found reality. It is the reality of things we do ourselves. It is not the abstract reality of your Christian teaching. It is the concrete, physical hereness of our reality. We know we can do all things. We know what we can do, no one can take that from us, because we will not permit it. We will defend our reality to the death. It is ourselves.[2]

On the other hand, intellectuals, including Russian scientists, have found the Communist philosophy and regime stifling and have taken drastic steps to escape from its influence. Dr. Mikhail Antonovich Klochko, a Soviet scientist who defected to the West during the summer of 1961, made a statement in a Canadian news conference in which he said:

> My name is Klochko, Mikhail Antonovich. I was born in the region of Poltava in the Ukraine in 1902, and I have lived in Russia all my life.
>
> I am a chemistry graduate of the Kiev Polytechnic Institute since 1925. I graduated with honors and remained at the institute as a teacher and research scientist. . . .
>
> I decided to leave the U.S.S.R. five years ago. It became impossible for me to bring to realization the scientific projects on which I was working. This was due to many factors.
>
> I was depressed by the lack of contact with the outside world, the falsity of information, and the difficulty of self expression.
>
> It became obvious to me that if I stayed in the U.S.S.R. I would not be able to give to mankind all that I could if I were in a free, democratic country.

I am now an old man and I am afraid of nothing, and I do not want my life work to be wasted. I feel that it will not be wasted here and I know that it would have been wasted in the U.S.S.R.

Nobody tempted me here. I was not tempted by any material considerations, but was forced to take this action to seek freedom of scientific expression and to save what is left of my human self-respect. . . .

It is the lack of human dignity in the U.S.S.R. that hurts most. I am not after fame or glory. I seek neither. I just want to serve mankind. I assure you that these are my full and real reasons, and this is my firm and final decision. . . . [3]

A Plan of Action

Communism provides a well-organized plan of action that enlists a quick response from the suffering and underprivileged who have been disillusioned by the unfulfilled promises of other programs and who look to this revolutionary movement as their last desperate hope. Communism feeds on discontent and poses as the champion of every oppressed group. Communists tell members of racial minorities that in Russia all racial discrimination has been eliminated. Actually, the Russian government has nurtured racial antagonisms when they served its purpose and has deliberately set group to fight against group when communism could profit from such conflict.

Communists urge colonial peoples to strive for independence as long as they are under the rule of non-Communist powers. They encourage crusaders for women's rights to believe that the Communist Party alone can give women real freedom. They impress the poor and the semistarved with the claim that communism is the only world-wide movement with both the determination and the organization to bring them help.

The vigorous action of communism has a strong appeal, which is illustrated by events a few years ago in a village of steelworkers. When the men started to climb the hill to work one morning, everyone in the village was happy for that day they were to pay the final installments on their homes. These families had sacrificed and skimped for years, and that day was to see the fulfillment of their dreams. Little did the wives realize that their husbands were going to the mill that morning for the last time.

That night when the day's work was done, the workers were told that the steel mill was closing. The company had decided to move the entire plant down to the coast nearer to the ships that brought the iron ore from across the seas. The homes of the villagers were their own, to be sure, but to what avail? Without jobs for the men, house values would drop to almost nothing, and despair took possession of the village.

Is it any wonder that this village became known as a hotbed of violence and revolution? Or is it surprising that the villagers responded eagerly when a group of men came to them with such slogans as: "Equality for all!" "Every man has a right to work!" "Act today for a better tomorrow!" The most urgent factor in this case was human need, human need for economic security, for escape from the paralyzing fear of poverty and unemployment, and from the desperate feeling that there was simply no other way out. Communism offered the only hope that their problems could be solved.

Beyond Self

It is not always personal interest that leads a man to accept communism. There are also those who are moved with compassion for the underprivileged though they themselves are living in fairly fortunate circumstances. Many well-educated people are found in this group. A good example is the noted French writer, André Gide, who once said:

> Why do I long for communism? Because I believe it to be equitable and because I suffer on account of the injustices which I feel more strongly than ever when it is myself who am favored. . . . Because I believe that through it we shall be able to reach the highest culture and because it is communism which can indeed most promote a new and better form of civilization. . . . What brought me to communism with my whole heart was the fact of the privileged position which I personally enjoyed that seemed to be preposterous and intolerable. I once had occasion to talk with one of the shipwrecked survivors of "La Bourgogne," and he told me that he had been lucky enough

to get into a lifeboat in which a number of men had got away; if more had been taken in, the boat would have capsized and sunk. The men in safety on board, armed with jackknives and hatchets, had hacked off the hands of those who, clinging to the sides of the boat, were endeavoring to scramble in out of the sea. The knowledge of being one of those in the lifeboat, of being safe, whilst others around me are drowning, that feeling became intolerable for me.[4]

André Gide was an idealist who felt that he had no right to live in better conditions than other men but was frustrated in his efforts to change things in the system of society of his day. Therefore he became convinced that communism could bring about a more just equality and more fair distribution of this world's goods. Gide was later disillusioned and took his place in the ranks of those who abandoned the Communist cause, but his statement serves to show how an intellectual may be led to support this movement.

Where Have Christians Failed?

When we observe the power with which communism has drawn into its ranks some of the good minds of our day, we are inclined to ask why such men and women have given themselves to communism rather than to Christianity. What is lacking in the present-day interpretation and expression of Christianity? Was not Christ concerned about the hungry, the sick, the friendless? Have not his followers always "ministered in his name"?

Surely the Bible does not lack social motivation. The prophets were constantly crying out against injustice and oppression, while our Lord declared himself to be the fulfillment of Isaiah's ringing words:

> The Spirit of the Lord is upon me,
> because he has anointed me to preach
>   good news to the poor.
> He has sent me to proclaim release to
>   the captives
> and recovering of sight to the blind,
> to set at liberty those who are op-
>   pressed. . . .   Luke 4:18-19

[7]

Christ and the church have historically denounced the same evils that communism decries. Furthermore, the Christian faith has the power to meet the needs of the empty and futile lives that masses of men lead today. It has made life worth living for people in all parts of the world and given them purpose and power. Nevertheless, the inaction of many Christians, the self-satisfaction of numerous others, and the frequent lack of an adequate, forward-looking program on the part of the church have led many persons to seek elsewhere for an answer to life's problems. In a real sense, nominal Christians share responsibility for the growth of the Communist movement.

This Handbook seeks to help Christians understand the sources of Communist strength and see the methods it uses. It recognizes the falsity of many Communist promises and the denial in practice of many of communism's idealistic goals. The informed Christian is not afraid to examine claims made by Communists or to judge their performance. This informed Christian knows that he must show Christlike compassion in action to needy people everywhere. He is convinced that the Christian answer is the only real solution of the world's suffering and despair.

Chapter 2 | Communism in Theory

Communism is a religion without God, a religion of men and machines. It is embodied today in a political and economic system with a totalitarian power that dominates Russia, the largest nation in Europe, and China, the nation with the largest population in the world. It has reached out to make converts and seize control of the government in other countries in Europe and Asia. It is making inroads in still other countries on these continents and in Latin America and Africa. The form that the expression of the principles of communism takes and the nature of its practices vary from country to country, from era to era, and with the shift of events from one part of the world to another. The many aspects of this powerful movement call for careful consideration.

A Theory of History

The originator of communism was Karl Marx who was born into a Jewish family in Rhenish Prussia in 1818 and baptized as a Protestant with his entire family when he was six years of age. He spent most of his life (1818-1883) in Germany and England, and, drawing many of his ideas from the German philosopher Friedrich Hegel, he developed a theory based on two characteristic features of the society he saw in those countries: (1) confidence in science as the key to unlock all mysteries of the universe and (2) class struggle between capitalists and laborers in the expanding industry of the period. From impressions along these lines, Marx and his friend Friedrich Engels developed a theory that Marx claimed was the chief of all sciences. He called it the "science of history," a theory of the movements of struggle and death in old systems of society and the birth of new systems that make up the continued story of the human race.

Marx declared that all human history is determined by the way men make their living and their ownership of tools to make that living. The conditions of production determine everything else that man has: government, art, social customs, even religion. Everything rests on the "forces of production" and knowledge of their use; they are the foundation of the economic system. This interpretation of history explained much of the human story, which before Marx's time had not been understood or appreciated. Christians, who believe that God is just as concerned about and active in man's economic life as he is in man's social, artistic, or intellectual life, are challenged by the truth in the insights of this nineteenth century scholar.

Marx said that the history of economic systems shows a definite pattern of development, which proceeds according to laws that he set forth. First there is a given system of society, which he calls the thesis. Then along comes a newer and opposed system, called the antithesis. These two struggle together until out of their struggle comes a third system, the synthesis. But soon the synthesis itself will be challenged. Then it will become a new thesis, which will be challenged by another antithesis that must struggle with it until a further synthesis develops. Such continued struggle is the development of history, according to Marx and the philosopher Hegel.

Actually, while Marx's theory explains well some points in history, it is an oversimplification and when it is clamped down on the whole human story, it hides quite as much as it reveals. Its insistence on development by opposing forces seems to prove that real progress in history can be achieved only through bloodshed and violence because at each stage the state is run by a ruling class that refuses to give up its power without a bitter struggle.

According to this theory the system of capitalism rose in opposition to the old feudal order and emphasized two new classes of people. First came the organizers of industry, the people with money who buy machines and build factories and use what the factories earn to buy more machines and build more factories.

[10]

These people are called capitalists because they work with accumulated money, or capital, to organize industry. Then there are the workers of industry, the people who run the machines in the factories. They have no money to invest, but they can sell their own work to capitalists who pay them wages for it. Industrial workers Marx called proletarians or the proletariat. The capitalists at that time were the masters of society, but capitalism, in turn, had its own contradictions. Capitalists must struggle with proletarians who represented to Marx a new system, and as time went on that struggle would grow fiercer. The capitalist system, according to Marx, was producing the very persons who would finally overthrow it.

An Economic Theory

Marx analyzed those features of capitalism that he said would lead to its destruction. He began with what is called the labor theory of value. According to this theory, he claimed the work that men do creates everything of value in the world. Things that man can have without any work, such as air and water, have no commercial value. Machines used to make valuable articles are themselves only the result of other men's labor. Actually they can produce nothing by themselves. In factories it is not the machines but the labor of the workingmen that creates the value of the product.

Yet the workingmen, Marx pointed out, do not receive the full value for the products they make. Part of that value is kept by the capitalists who own the factories, and this they call their profit. Marx called it the surplus value. Because the capitalists keep this surplus value or profit, Marx believed that they were actually robbing the workers of what should by right be theirs.

More machines and larger factories, Marx reasoned, will mean more profits for the capitalists. Larger business organizations and ever larger factories will emerge, he said, because each capitalist will seek to drive his competitors out of business. The result will be that all but a few capitalists will be forced out of business and those remaining will establish monopolies that will control most of the economic life of the country. The capitalist class, therefore, will get smaller and smaller while the proletariat will become larger until it includes practically the whole population. When that stage is reached, Marx prophesied, the capitalists will not be able to withstand the workers any longer.

As the capitalists become fewer, they will also become wealthier because each of them will be receiving more profits, Marx asserted. The condition of the workers, on the other hand, would not improve. Unemployment and depressions would increase their misery.

Because the workers are not paid the full value of the things they make, they cannot buy all the things that the factories are producing. Therefore, unsold products will pile up and up. Capitalists will try for a time to get rid of these stockpiles by forcing them on backward countries, and the result will be imperialistic wars and conquest. Finally the time will come when the surplus simply cannot be sold and so the capitalist will have to close his factory and stop producing new things until he can get rid of the goods that he has on hand in his inventory. When thousands of factories do this, the result will be a general depression with millions of men thrown out of work and the whole economic system at a standstill.

It should be noted that much of Marx's reasoning is a neat exercise in deductive logic that sounds very persuasive and logical but actually overlooks or ignores the evidence and complexity of history. Marxism oversimplifies, misunderstands, and distorts the nature of value, profits, the impact of technology on society, and the nature of society, government, man, and the "surplus value." It fails to comprehend the complexity of modern depressions and the causes of war.

Under no system can the worker buy all the things that factories are producing, because part of his own production goes to pay for medical, educational, governmental, business, and other services he needs. Even in the Soviet Union, the worker receives only a small share of the value of what he produces. That is why the difference between "full value" and "wages" does not normally produce surpluses that pile up and cannot be sold. Every economic system, including both capitalist and Communist, has a tendency to consume what it produces, exchanging some of its production with other nations. The prosperity of a nation does not depend upon the amount of money it has but upon the per capita amount of goods and services its citizens have.

Genuine surpluses rarely exist during the growth of an industrial society. They tend to appear only when industrialization has reached a mature development. At that stage the rate of growth of an economy slows down and shifts toward a saturation level for certain produced goods and services. When the demand for any item is largely satisfied, the new level of technology permits an increase in leisure time, which gradually spreads through the entire economy. It is not accidental that working hours have been steadily decreasing while real income has been increasing since the coming of the Industrial Revolution.

America has already reached this maturity in a number of industries. The surpluses in farm products and a few other commodities have not produced a depression, and they certainly are not the cause of recent wars. A slow adjustment is taking place under indirect controls exercised by the government, using "government" in the American sense of elected representatives of a free people acting together responsibly. Such government seeks to stabilize the production of some commodities and to expand in new directions, inducing people to shift freely into new kinds of work for which there is a greater demand by the nation as a whole. The result, in the long run, is more leisure for all. Marx could not be aware of the relationship to develop between technological growth and capital investment and the increasing prosperity and leisure to come under the system he termed "capitalism." On the contrary, by his system of reasoning he predicted increasing misery for the worker.

The general growth curve of an industry, however, should not be confused with the cyclical fluctuations within the curve itself. In the short run, cyclical depressions seem to be caused mainly by the difficulty in a free economy of maintaining a steady rate of investment, by the absence of inventions, and by the changing psychology of buyers and sellers.

A searching examination of the American economy today leads to the conclusion that it has little in common with the old-fashioned European capitalism of 1848 when Marx was writing. In many ways the "capitalism" that Communists constantly decry today is gone in the West, and a new and different economic system better called "democratic enterprise" has taken its place.

The new "capitalism" has created a vast productive machinery that is capable of supporting the wants of a growing population, and this, in turn, has supplied more jobs, better pay, and more

[13]

favorable working conditions. The benefits achieved by labor unions, such as the shorter work week, paid vacations, pensions and a better working environment were unknown in the nineteenth century and are still not enjoyed in many parts of the world. While improvements are still needed in many places, the old capitalism has been left behind at many points.

Many of the imperfections of the "democratic enterprise" system stem from difficulties arising from an intricate monetary and credit system rather than from the profit motive as such. No economic system ever has been or ever will be perfect, and continuous efforts are being made to improve peacefully present practices.

Marx recognized in his later works some of the difficulties indicated above and tried to get around them but with no great success. Economists generally have found his theories inadequate and have rejected them.

Actual developments have proved that Marx was also wrong in thinking that under "capitalism" the lot of the workers would become worse and worse. He did not reckon with the trade union movement, which, combined with increased productivity, has made the lot of the worker better with ever higher wages and better living conditions as democratic enterprise has advanced. Nor did he foresee that government regulations would prevent the full development of the monopolies he predicted or that government planning would seek to curb unemployment.

The Communist theory of imperialism has also been shown to be a dangerous half-truth. It explains some of the imperialistic actions of nations during the past century, but there are many that it does not explain. Imperialism existed long before capitalism, as the eras of Caesar, Alexander, and the Pharaohs attest, and it exists also under communism. The desire for power over one's fellow men is just as strong a desire as that for economic gain, and, therefore, imperialism can never be understood simply in terms of economics.

Every group knows the efforts that men make simply to get power, and on the international level this plays as big a part in imperialism as any search for markets. It is clear that many individuals have been interested in markets and greater production for the sake of piling up money and that such money can be used responsibly. Evidence is seen in the rise of foundations to help

[14]

uild and run schools, hospitals, and libraries throughout the world and to encourage science and research.

The narrowness of the Communist theory of imperialism only succeeds in blinding the eyes of Communists to their own particular form of imperialism. It is impossible for them to admit that they were guilty of imperialistic action in cases like their entry into Tibet and Hungary.

The Way to an Ideal Society

"Workers of the world unite; you have nothing to lose but your chains" was Marx's battle cry in the middle of the nineteenth century. The proletariat, he declared, will seize the government and then by means of government power take possession of the factories and run them for the good of all rather than for the profit of the few. The government will own all the means of production—land, tools, factories. Because everything is controlled by the government there can be careful planning to see that production actually meets the needs of the people.

Heretofore, contended Marx, the government has always been an agency for the members of the ruling class, preserving their property rights and special privileges. It is no more than a committee of property owners whose function is to hold down the workers. When the revolution comes and the workers take over, he promised, the new government will be for the good of all, including the workers who make up practically the whole population.

The coming of this revolution Marx believed to be inevitable. The role of the Communists was only to show the workers what they must do and to hasten the day when the workers would revolt and crush their oppressors. This is the march of history, said Marx, the inevitable "scientific" evolution of the human race.

After the revolution, continued Marx, the proletarians, now liberated, will become the liberators of all. They will take the gains of science and industry, developed through the so-called capitalistic era, and make them serve mankind. There will be no more exploitation of one class by another because all men will belong to the same class. Since private property, which is the root of exploitation and all injustice, will have disappeared, evil itself will disappear. In this new type of society, there will be true communism, the free sharing of all by everyone. Science and industry, used for the common good, will provide an abundance of benefits.

And so, said Marx, history will reach its climax and be stabilized. There will be no more struggle, no more thesis, antithesis, and synthesis for there will be no classes to struggle with each other. The classless Communist society will be the final synthesis of all. Lenin, Marx's greatest disciple, described that final state in these words:

> And then will democracy itself begin to wither away due to the simple facts that freed from capitalistic slavery, from the untold horrors, savageries, and infamies of the capitalistic exploitation, people will gradually become accustomed to the observance of the elemental rules of social life that have been known for centuries and repeated for thousands of years in all schoolbooks; they will become accustomed to observing them without force, without compulsion, with subordination, and without the special apparatus for compulsion which is called the state.[1]

On the basis of Marx's view of economic life, Soviet leaders set out late in the nineteenth and early in the twentieth century to guide men in their steps to the better future they promised. They called on the workers to remedy their ills, not by gradual methods like trade unionism, broad private investment, and government but by violent revolution.

Karl Marx died in 1883. By 1890, Nikolai Lenin (1870-1924), a confirmed Marxist, was the leader of the radical Social Democrats in Russia. In 1903, at the Second Congress of the Communist Party, Lenin led the Bolsheviks (meaning the majority) who issued at that Congress the first program of the Communist Party. The goals of this program were the overthrow of the czarist autocracy in Russia and the bourgeois–landlord system and the establishment of the dictatorship of the proletariat. Thus with passion and definite plans for action, Lenin set into motion the philosophy of Marx.

A Power Movement

Russo-Communism has embodied Marx's theories in a closely organized movement of tremendous power. This fact is due largely to the skill and genius of Lenin who determined that the Communist Party should be organized like an army with strict obedience and unquestioning loyalty to those in positions of leadership. He used this army–like organization on November 6, 1917, to seize power in Russia. With it he destroyed the only democratic government Russia ever had, a Socialist regime set up after the abdication of the Czar on March 15, 1917.

Lenin's principal enemies were not the Czar and capitalism. His real fight was against Socialists and socialism. He had to get rid of them before he could set up the kind of totalitarian rule for the whole country that he had previously established in the party.

Under Lenin's leadership the Communist parties throughout the world were united, and rigid adherence to orders from Moscow was enforced by propaganda, political intrigue, and police terror. This continued in Stalin's era (1924-1953).

The completeness of Moscow's control of the Communist Party in other countries was evident in the days of the Nazi–Soviet pact. In 1939 when this pact was signed, the Communists, who for years had been campaigning for a united front against fascism, suddenly dropped this campaign and became advocates of keeping peace with fascism in order to unleash World War II.

Stalin, who had succeeded Lenin in 1924, planned to take over Europe after England and Germany had bled each other to death. Then suddenly in 1941 when Hitler attacked Russia, the Communist parties reversed their position within a day's time, dropped all their peace movements, and came all-out for war against fascism. Even in countries that were under foreign rule, where they had always opposed conquerors and their "imperialist wars," Communists became loyal supporters of the government and did everything to further the war effort.

Since World War II a similar subservience to Moscow on the part of Communist parties in satellite and other countries has continued. There can be much disagreement among the leaders within a national Communist party, but as long as that leadership keeps the confidence of Moscow, it stays in power. Once it loses that confidence, there is trouble.

Some differences of opinion between Russia and China and Russia and other countries are, however, now beginning to come out in the open. Mao Tse-tung of China and his regime are challenging some of Khrushchev's actions. The Twenty-Second Congress of the Communist Party in Moscow in October, 1961, brought out very clearly such disagreement. This may indicate that practices in the nineteen-fifties, such as change in leadership and policy in Communist parties in India and Japan after attacks by Moscow, may change. Divergencies among Communist parties, such as those apparent today in Poland, Yugoslavia, Russia, and China, may lead to developments that will change the international scene.

Methods of Working

Communism has ways by which its followers carry out long-range programs, achieve well-defined goals, and infiltrate other groups. Communists are skillful in the use of propaganda, keeping up a constant stream of it, but they are not interested in getting out well-reasoned and factual documents. They may be either for or against peace—whichever seems the best strategy for their cause at the time. They call names and use rousing slogans that demand immediate action, thus appealing to those who have no patience for more gradual processes. They try to control newspapers and magazines and to work their way into places of influence on the editorial boards of all sorts of publications and other propaganda vehicles. Anyone who reads regularly a Communist publication will quickly come to recognize certain routine slogans and catchwords that reveal clearly what Communists are currently for or against.

Communists carry on indoctrination projects, using names that stand for something very different in the history and traditions of the country. Schools established by Communists in the United States were given the names "Jefferson School," "Adams School," and "Lincoln School" although Thomas Jefferson, John Adams, and Abraham Lincoln would have had nothing to do with their teachings. The first step of Communists is not usually open attack but sowing of seeds of distrust about people or organizations that oppose them. It does not matter to the Communist that what he says and teaches is not true.

Communists also use techniques of confusion. They fear Socialists far more than people on "the right" because they believe that middle-of-the-road people have much more chance of winning support and defeating the Communist program than conservatives. In order to put moderately liberal people into a bad light with conservative groups, Communists often identify themselves with them, get them labeled "red" or at least "pink," and so create distrust and confusion. Another technique of confusion is to make it appear that anyone who opposes communism is against social security, racial equality, or some other good cause that is advocated by others as well as by Communists.

Formation of "secret" cells, often called study groups, is a favored Communist practice. The encouragement given to cell members never to be honest or frank with those outside the cell group produces a gradual disintegration of the sense of truth and honesty and breaks down the feeling that truth is necessary in human relationships as a basis for holding society together. The purpose of a study course that may start with some objective social reform is to make the cell members feel critical of their own society to the extent that they lose faith in betterment coming through peaceful change. At the same time, Communist ideologies are presented in an uncritical light with emphasis on the ideal society, which Communists claim they can create, rather than a critical study of the up-to-date accomplishments of the Communist movement, the means used, and what the results are likely to be.

The cell inculcates the idea of obedience to senior party members and insists on loyalty to party leaders rather than to principles clearly presented and discussed. In the beginning at least, cell members do not usually understand that the real object of the cell is to train members for the Communist Party, and often they do not know that the cell is Communist led. The cell often gets such a hold of an individual's life and thought that he feels he is nothing apart from his cell group and becomes completely dependent on it.

In the United States at the present time communism and cell-type of activity is at a minimum, at least above ground. A great deal of espionage may be going on below the surface. The party is not barred legally from political activity, including speaking in public, but it is required by the Internal Security Law, passed in 1950 and supported by the Supreme Court in 1961, to register as an arm of the Soviet Union. Heavy fines and imprisonment of leaders may be imposed for refusal to register by a set date, a requirement that the party opposes vigorously. One estimate of the party's strength in the United States was that there are now fewer than five thousand members, with an average age past fifty. Other sources claim a membership of ten thousand.

Various organizations for adults and youth are active in Communist nations. They have names that appeal to the idealistic such as "The People's Committee for Peace" or "Committee for World Youth Friendship and Cultural Exchange." As soon as it becomes known that such an organization is Communist led, the name is changed. Only about one-fourth of the sponsors whose names appear on the letterheads of these organizations are Communists. The others are unsuspecting people of good reputation asked to lend their names as sponsors of some worthy cause.

Communists advocate united front activities in labor unions, political groups, and other organizations. The Communists may be in the minority, but a small group will outmaneuver the other persons at a meeting, appealing to the majority desire to do things in a parliamentary way. The alternatives are to put a time limit on debate or to outsit and outwit the Communist group who have long used such techniques to wear their opponents down. After enough persons have left the meeting to give them a majority, Communists will let an issue come to a vote. They are tireless workers who can be matched only by workers more tireless than they.

When instigating strikes or working with grievance committees in schools, Communists, in many instances, are not really trying to get better conditions within a situation. They are trying to create confusion and break down the existing system. This makes it impossible to work with them even though their aims appear to be the same as those of responsible reformers.

In satellite countries like Hungary and East Germany where the party's drive for power succeeds, it establishes a dictatorship even more rigid than that of the party. Lenin and his successor Stalin, far more than Marx, emphasized that the dictatorship of the proletariat is to be an intermediate step after the Communists gain power. This dictatorship will end when Communists are able to bring in the ideal society they expect to establish. In this intermediate period the power of the government under Communist control, which is expected eventually to wither away, is made stronger in order to fight the vestiges of the system supplanted. This power of Communist government is used even against the workers. Thus the dictatorship of the proletariat turns out to be a dictatorship by the leaders of the party, and they have to invent ever stricter controls even over the workers.

This intermediate stage of dictatorship began in Russia in 1917 and has continued to the present. Communists say that the reason for this is that there is always danger of war between Communist and "capitalist" countries; the dictatorship stage cannot be ended until all the world is Communist. The Soviet Party's Draft Program, prepared for submission to the Twenty-Second Congress of the Soviet Communist Party in October, 1961, Part Two, Section 3, describes the present situation in the U.S.S.R. in these words:

> The dictatorship of the proletariat, born of the Socialist revolution, has played an epoch-making role by insuring the victory of socialism in the U.S.S.R. In the course of Socialist construction, however, it underwent changes. After the exploiting classes had been abolished, the state function of suppressing their resistance ceased to exist. The chief functions of the Socialist state—economic and organizational, cultural and educational—have developed in full measure. The Socialist state has entered a new phase.
>
> The state has begun to grow over into a nationwide organization of the working people of Socialist society. . . . Having brought about a complete and final victory of socialism—the first phase of communism—and the transition of society to the full-scale construction of communism, the dictatorship of the proletariat has fulfilled its historic mission and has ceased to be indispensable in the U.S.S.R. from the point of view of the tasks of internal development. . . .
>
> The state, which arose as a state of the dictatorship of the proletariat, has become a state of the entire people, an organ expressing the interests and will of the people as a whole. Since the working class is the foremost and best organized force of Soviet society, it plays a leading role also in the period of the full-scale construction of communism. The working class will

[21]

have completed its function of leader of society after communism is built and classes disappear.

The party holds that the dictatorship of the working class will cease to be necessary before the state withers away. The state as an organization embracing the entire people will survive until the complete victory of communism.[2]

A Religion

But communism is far more than a theory of history or economics, the way to an ideal society or a power movement. It must also be regarded as a religion. This seems strange since it believes in materialism and teaches that there is no God. Marx believed that matter is the only final reality and that both ideals and ideas are just products of matter in motion. He denied, and communism still denies, the existence of any point of reference outside the material world. There is no creator, no human soul, no eternal life, no divine law. If communism denies all this, how can it be a religion?

Basically communism is a religion because it offers a framework for man's understanding of himself, of the world, and of man's place in the world. It has its own teaching about the fundamental nature of existence and of the world. It has its own teaching about the purpose of life in the world, the life of individuals, and the life of the human race. It professes to meet the fundamental problems of life and so must be regarded as a religion.

Communism is also a religion because it demands a man's ultimate loyalty. It expects the kind of absolute allegiance and dedication with passion from its followers that Christians can give only to God. It provides its followers with a philosophy; a faith to live by with dedicated devotion; a program of action; and hope for the establishment of the final good for mankind. This final good, this perfect society-to-be, takes the place of the Kingdom of God in men's thoughts. The writings of Marx and Lenin take the place of the Bible as the Communist's source of authority, and anyone who disagrees with Marx and Lenin is regarded as a heretic to be eliminated at all costs.

While communism acknowledges the reality of evil, it teaches that its origin is in personal ownership of private property and that when such ownership has been abolished by state ownership of natural resources and the means of production and when all men share equally the products of their labor, the source of sin will have been removed and a perfect society will be possible. Man by his own efforts will have ended sin. Communism sees the source of evil outside of man—in the economic system—and the source of salvation within man—in communism. Christianity finds the source of evil within man himself and the source of salvation outside of man—in God.

As a Whole

Nikita Khrushchev, in presenting the third program of the Communist Party to the delegates at the Twenty-second Congress, defined communism in these words:

> Communism is a classless social system with one form of public ownership of the means of production and full social equality of all members of society; under it, the all around development of people will be accompanied by the growth of the productive forces through continuous progress in science and technology, all sources of public wealth will gush forth abundantly, and the great principle, "From each according to his ability, to each according to his needs," will be implemented. Communism is a highly organized society of free, socially conscious working people in which self-government will be established, in which labor for the good of society will become the prime and vital requirement of everyone, a necessity recognized by one and all, and the ability of each person will be employed to the greatest benefit of the people.[3]

Taken as a whole, communism is a conglomeration of philosophy, economic theory and practice, totalitarian techniques, and wholehearted commitment. The various elements have no logical relationship to one another. Communists have been held together by overpowering personalities and a passion for their cause rather than by a unified, logical set of principles expressed in a consistent way.

Communist theory ignores men's pride and desire for power and their ingrained selfishness and assumes that if all have an abundance of jointly owned wealth, these sources of evil will disappear.

The broad scope of Communist claims is part of the party's attraction and power. The Marxian explanation of how men live and work together appeals to those who want a simple and final solution for all life's problems. But the Christian still asks the Communist, "Can man live by bread alone? Can man live without God?"

Chapter 3	# Communism in Practice

On October 17, 1961, the Twenty-Second Congress of the Soviet Communist Party opened in a new marble-and-glass palace in the Kremlin in Moscow. In addition to delegates from the Union of Soviet Socialist Republics, representatives of some eighty foreign countries were present together with guests from the U.S.S.R. and several African and Asian countries. The announced attendance was almost five thousand, and the delegates claimed to represent thirty million people.

Sixty-three years before, in March, 1898, nine delegates representing six Communist party organizations met secretly in much more modest quarters in Minsk, Russia, and laid plans for a Marxist organization that would eventually rule Russia. Five years later, in 1903, at its Second Congress, the Communist Party, adopted its first program, the goal the overthrow of the Czar and of the bourgeoisie–landlord system and the establishment of the "dictatorship of the proletariat." In 1919, this goal attained, the Eighth Congress approved a second party program, its goal a Socialist society. Five-year plan succeeded five-year plan until in 1961 Nikita Khrushchev, First Secretary of the Communist Party and Premier of the Union of Soviet Socialist Republics, could claim that the goal of a Socialist society had been reached. The second program of the party had been carried out, and the main business of the October, 1961, Twenty-Second Congress was the approval of the third program. In the draft of this program published in the summer preceding the Congress, Khrushchev said:

. . . A mighty unifying thunderstorm marking the springtime of mankind is raging over the earth. The Socialist revolution has resulted in the establishment of the world Socialist system. A powerful wave of national liberation revolutions is sweeping away the colonial system of imperialism.

One-third of mankind is building a new life under the banner of scientific communism. . . . The Socialist world is expanding; the capitalist world is shrinking. Socialism will inevitably succeed capitalism everywhere. . . .

The supreme goal of the party is to build a Communist society on whose banner will be inscribed "From each according to his ability, to each according to his needs." The party's motto "Everything in the name of man for the benefit of man" will be put into effect in full. . . .

The great October Revolution breached the imperialist front in Russia, one of the world's largest countries, firmly established the dictatorship of the proletariat, created a new type of state—the Soviet state—and a new type of democracy—democracy for the working people.[1]

Against this background of the aims and achievements of the Communist Party, this chapter is a quick review of some Communist practices in the U.S.S.R. over more than four decades and in other parts of the world.

In the Union of Soviet Socialist Republics

Politics

The U.S.S.R. is a highly centralized federation of fifteen republics, which spreads out over 8,500,000 square miles or one-sixth of the surface of the globe and administers the affairs of over 216 million citizens. The members of the Supreme Soviet, which is the highest legislative authority of the Soviet Union, are "elected" by universal suffrage. The people have the "secret ballot" in these elections, but there are no opposition candidates. A vote supporting the government is cast simply by dropping the ballot into the box, while a vote against the government requires going into a voting booth to mark the ballot. The voter identifies himself with his passport, and it is easy for party officials to check off the few names of those using the booth. Each republic, region, city, and village also has a soviet or council. In practice these soviets have become a facade behind which the Communist Party exercises absolute control.

The Supreme Soviet, which meets twice a year, is a parliament with two houses. Its duties are to approve the budget and to appoint important committees to which its authority is delegated. In addition, in recent years, the Supreme Soviet has rubber-stamped all important policy decisions in such areas as educational reform, new criminal and court legislation, the MTS (Machine Tractor Station) reform, and economic plans. The Presidium and the Council of Ministers are permanent standing committees of the Supreme Soviet with authority between sessions of the Soviet to interpret laws, issue edicts, and appoint or remove officials. Nikita Khrushchev is chairman of the Council of Ministers, the body with most power, as well as Premier.

Parallel to the government is the Communist Party organization which is active throughout the country. This is the only political party that is legal in the U.S.S.R. Its membership in 1961, as announced at the Twenty-Second Congress, was 9,716,005, an increase of 2,500,000 since the Twentieth Congress in 1956.

The Communist Party looks to the party Congress for final authority. Between sessions of the Congress, the party turns over its power to the Central Committee, which now has 175 full members and meets about twice a year. This Central Committee selects the party secretariat and its own Presidium, The Presidium, formerly called the Politbureau, is the most powerful group of its size in the world. All the principal party secretaries are members, including the First Secretary—at the present time Premier Nikita S. Khrushchev. The Presidium elected in October, 1961, has eleven full members and five alternate members.

On the top levels of both the Soviet State and the Communist Party, the same men are to be found. The two systems are thus linked into a highly organized, interlocking dictatorship. Through its complete control of political, social, educational, economic, and military spheres of life, the party is able to dominate the lives of all the citizens of the Soviet Union, although its membership includes less than 5 per cent of the population. The party is

[27]

a very exclusive body and not many can qualify for membership. As a special reward for their spectacular space journeys, the two Soviet cosmonauts—Major Gherman S. Titov and Major Yuri A. Gagarin—were made delegates to the Twenty-Second Congress and were greeted with hearty applause.

Altogether this monolithic, totalitarian government is able to maintain itself in power through its centralized organization, secret police, control of the press and other forms of communication, public services promised and widely publicized, and constant propaganda supporting its views and actions.

Police, the KGB

No description of the government of the Soviet Union would be complete without reference to the political or secret police. Within a few weeks of the time they came to power, the Communists fashioned this instrument of control. Internal conflicts during succeeding years caused the government to maintain and enlarge this service, changing its name from time to time, and to charge it with dealing with fancied or real expressions of opposition and sabotage. This important agency of control was known until 1960 as the Ministry of Internal Affairs (MVD) and is now the Committee for State Security (KGB).

While the basic powers of the police still permit it to accomplish virtually anything it may wish if the regime orders an increase of repression at any time, the police structure has undergone reduction in its extraordinary powers of arrest, banishment, and enforced labor since the death of Stalin. Under Khrushchev, primitive forced labor camps for political prisoners have been greatly reduced if not abolished and relaxation of extreme oppression by police has created a far different scene than that of the Stalin era.

Economics

1. State Ownership

The outstanding feature in the economy of the Soviet Union is state ownership of the means of production such as land, minerals, waters, forests, factories, mills, mines, railroads, banks, and agriculture. In the nineteenth century, under the leadership of the Western countries, the dominant economic policy was that of nonintervention on the part of the state. In the twentieth century the Soviet Union has spearheaded an opposite trend, the active intervention of the state in the economy.

It is interesting to note that the West's policy of nonintervention by government has been modified considerably in recent years. The economy of the West is now influenced to a considerable degree by government but in no way comparable to the economy of the Soviet Union, which was taken over entirely long ago by the state. The whole Soviet Union has been transformed into one huge factory. The free play of the market, with its emphasis upon supply and demand, is no longer a controlling factor in the Soviet economy.

There are two planning commissions called GOSPLAN and GOSEKONOMSOVIET, the first concerned with short-term, the second with long-term planning. They have set up economic goals to be achieved over successive plan periods. Such planning is based on party leadership directives. These goals establish priorities as well as the balance between heavy and light industries. The draft plans are submitted for review to regional and local units and, after occasional adjustments, are adopted as binding.

2. Industrialization

The second outstanding factor in the Soviet system is the impressive industrialization that has been achieved. After the Revolution Russia set out deliberately—regardless of human cost—to become a modern industrial nation. As the least developed of the great European powers, but rich in natural resources, the country gradually expanded the industrialization begun in the eighteen-eighties. In 1914, czarist Russia had reached the level of French production in heavy industry. By 1941, Soviet heavy industry reached equality with that of Germany.

Since World War II this industrialization has proceeded rapidly. Thousands of factories of all types have been erected up and down the land. The most modern techniques and processes have been introduced on a wide scale, though the old ways of doing things, especially in agriculture, still prevail in many places. The Soviet Union stands today as the second greatest industrial power on earth, accounting for almost one-fifth of the world's industrial output. This output, Khrushchev claimed at the Twenty-Second Congress, amounts to more than 60 per cent of the output of the United States. He also said that in the last three years

Soviet industrial output has been rising at an average of 10.2 per cent compared with the United States growth of 2.3 per cent. He promised that heavy industry would continue to play a leading role in the Soviet economy.

From 1929 to 1959 the output of cotton cloth merely doubled, and woolen cloth increased less than four times during a period when the population using these products grew by more than 40 per cent. Only 13 per cent of the total industrial investment of the U.S.S.R. from 1918 to 1959 went to industries producing consumer goods. The remaining 87 per cent was invested in capital-goods-producing industries, according to the Statistical Yearbook, National Economy of the U.S.S.R., published in Russian in 1959 by the Central Statistical Administration. No other nation has ever had so unbalanced an industrial development.

It is true, however, that consumer goods have increased in recent years. For the most part, however, their production remains a goal for the future. Khrushchev has promised the Soviet people a greatly improved standard of living by 1980. The increases in production goals for consumer goods match those for heavy industry.

At the Twenty-Second Congress Mr. Khrushchev stressed the fact that industrial plans have been for "peaceful construction" but maintained that the Communist Party never overlooks the need to strengthen the economic might of the country and its defenses. "We now have," he said, "at our disposal intercontinental ballistic missiles, anti-aircraft rocket equipment, and rockets for the land, naval, and air forces. A nuclear-powered submarine fleet is being built up and equipped with ballistic and target-seeking rockets."[2]

As early as 1920 Lenin foresaw the necessity of developing electric power and wrote that "socialism plus electrification equals communism." Huge hydroelectric and thermal power plants have sprung up throughout the country, sending out streams of power across the Soviet Union in all directions. In 1940, the output was almost twenty-four times that of 1913; in 1960, the reported output represented a sixfold increase over the 1940 figure and a 143-fold increase over the 1913 figure. The goal announced by Khrushchev for output by 1980 is 2,700 to 3,000 billions of kilowatt hours or 50 per cent more electric power than is now produced in all other countries. If this goal for 1980 is reached, the

Soviet Union's output of electric power in kilowatt hours will be 1,400 times that of prerevolutionary Russia.

It is claimed that the Volga hydroelectric station, named after Lenin, which has a capacity of 2.3 million kilowatts, is the largest such station in the world. Construction of new giant stations in Bratak on the Angara, Krasnoyarsk on the Yenissei and Stalingrad on the Volga—renamed Volgograd in late 1961—is scheduled for completion or near completion by 1965. The combined capacity of these three plants will be more than ten times larger than the capacity of all electric power stations in the Russia of 1913.

Agriculture

Another characteristic feature of communism is the collectivization of agriculture. The party government of Russia began this program in 1929, after it felt itself sufficiently strong to force its will upon an independent peasant class. The purpose of establishing collective farms was to have an instrument of political control over the individual peasant as well as to increase the supply of grain and foodstuffs directly available to the government for the growing urban and industrial population. The government had arrested, brutally treated, and exiled or executed thousands upon thousands of kulaks, farmers who profited from the labor of poorer peasants. The kulaks opposed Soviet policies, especially the collectivization of land, and were exceedingly antagonistic to the new regime.

Much pressure was brought to bear upon the peasants to force them onto collective farms. When their land was taken from them for the collectives, great numbers of peasants destroyed their crops and livestock with the result that masses were left by the government to starve. A reign of cruel repression covered vast areas of the countryside during the years of the change. Agricultural production suffered a catastrophic decline. Not till years later did crop production begin to regain its old level, and even today animal products (milk, meat, and eggs) lag behind the population growth.

Today Soviet agriculture is divided into three principal sectors: the collective farms (kolkhoz), the state farms (sovkhoz), and the private sector which is negligible in size.

The collective farm is the dominant form of agricultural organization, although state farms have become increasingly important in recent years. Collective farms differ from state farms in four ways. First, the collective—rather than the state—nominally owns all of the farm's productive assets other than land. This means all machinery, tools, and livestock. Second, the collective farm is financed largely from the profits of its own operations, the state farm from the state budget. Third, the collective farmer's wages are more dependent on the success of the crop than those of the state farmers. And, fourth, collective farms' produce is sold both at state stores, at relatively low, state-determined prices, and, after the farms' commitments to the state have been met, at collective farm markets at higher, free-market prices. The state farms produce almost entirely for state stores. Despite their small size, the intensively cultivated private plots of collective farm members, state farm members, industrial workers, and a few remaining individual peasants produce a significant share of the total agricultural output. Throughout the years of Soviet power—notwithstanding recent adjustments—the regime's agricultural price policy has been such that it extracted from agriculture, via low purchase prices paid to farmers by the state, huge "surplus value" for the financing of the government's ambitious investment programs.

Economic Effects

1. Economic Security

When the state controls all means of production, raw materials, market, and manpower, it can shift the emphasis according to need and thus avoid depressions. Consequently, the effects of unemployment have been eliminated. On the other hand, the Soviet worker is not so free to change his job as workers in the Western countries. He has privileges, such as a house that goes with his job, that are forfeited only at great sacrifice. To quit altogether is worse. The person who walks out on his job is as guilty of desertion as a soldier would be if he left the army of his own accord and subject to severe penalities. Any applicant for a job must submit his "work booklet" in which the entire record of his past employment is inscribed, including past violations of discipline and penalties incurred. And unless he left his last employment with authorization and documentary evidence, he is refused a job and, in many cases, turned over to the proper authorities for disciplining. Thus the worker in the Soviet Union has little freedom to improve his lot.

2. A Classless Society

Marxism makes much of the classless society when all people will belong to a great working-class family with everyone working for the welfare of the national family household. Of late, however, not so much stress has been laid on this phase. Although Khrushchev refers to communism as a "classless social system" in the draft of the program presented to the 1961 Congress, he calls attention to the emergence of a "new intelligentsia coming from the people and devoted to socialism." He further claims that "the common vital interests of the workers, peasants, and intellectuals have furnished a basis for indestructible socio-political and ideological unity of the Soviet people."

In addition to these three classes that can be clearly recognized are the ruling element, less important officials, and still lower party workers, engineers, and technicians. The French writer, André Gide, the ex-Communist quoted earlier, saw as he said "all the old layers of society forming again; if not precisely social classes, at least a new kind of aristocracy of right thinkers and conformists." "In the next generation," he suggested, "it may well be an aristocracy of money."

What is more, the lower classes have no right to organize to better their lot. The trade union movement, which in many lands has been the instrument for expressing and enforcing the demands of the laborers, is in Russia a branch of the government and devotes itself to securing harder work and greater productivity from the laborers.

3. Equality of Incomes

Communism first started in Russia on the principle that everyone should receive the same wage, but this was soon changed. The 1936 Constitution, Article 12, reads "From each according to his ability; to each according to his work." The change from the older Marxian formulation "To each according to his need" is striking, but Khrushchev quotes both statements with apparent approval in the 1961 Party Program Draft. Enormous variations in salaries and wages have arisen, far greater salary differentials than in the West. While so-called capitalist countries have been moving toward greater equality of income, the homeland of com-

[33]

munism has followed a trend in the opposite direction and now exhibits a degree of inequality comparable to that of major Western lands about the year 1900. All this, however, the program of the party adopted in 1961 promises optimistically to change.

4. Standard of Living

Controversy exists as to the degree to which living standards have changed under Communist rule. The regime's recent concessions to Soviet consumers reflect a desire to improve economic incentives and a concern for consumer welfare. To a considerable extent consumer goods, including the most elementary food articles, remain scarce and living standards have been kept from rising by deliberate policy. The regime has continued to foster the development of heavy industry in the interests of expanding the bases of economic and military power.

Crowded living conditions still exist, with many families occupying a single apartment, one family to a room. Even if the Soviet long-term housing program is carried out, there will be only nine square meters (about ninety-five square feet) of housing space available for every individual in the U.S.S.R. This is about the amount of space specified by nineteenth century hygienists as necessary to maintain health; it is also the norm currently required by law for prisons in the United States.

Much attention is given in the 1961 party program to the improvement of the standard of living in the years ahead. Declaring that there is now every possibility to improve rapidly the living standard of the entire population, the program foresees raising of wages according to quantity and quality of work, increases in distribution of public funds providing free education and medical treatment, pensions, and other services, and far-flung construction of dwellings and cultural and service buildings. Greater prosperity than that enjoyed in "capitalist" countries is assured with the shrinking of the disparity between high and comparatively low incomes. Of course it must be recognized that these are promises far beyond actual conditions today.

Social Aspects

1. Education

In the Soviet Union the whole cultural system is regarded as educational. The purpose, scope, and control of the educational system are different from that in non-Communist countries. Stalin is quoted as having said that education is a weapon whose effect depends upon who holds it in his hands and at whom it is aimed. The purpose of Communist education is definitely social and the ideal is to make a good Communist of each person and to mold a new generation into a Communist nation. The scope of such education embraces not only the formal educational program as it is understood in the West but also all possible means of imparting information and influencing others. The press, with its newspapers, magazines, and books, the radio, television, libraries, movies, and theatres are all a part of the system and are used to control the thinking of the people. No one can escape the continuous government educational propaganda. Rigid control over everything said in public is maintained by the Communist Party through its central organs.

Modern totalitarianism, to be effective, requires literacy in order that it may increase its control over the minds of men. The literacy rate in the Soviet Union has increased each decade until the current claim is 98.5 per cent. This, however, applies only to those between the ages of nine and forty-nine.

The number in school for the 1960-61 school year, according to Soviet claims, is 36,000,000 in general educational schools, which include schools for workers, rural youth, and adults; 540,-000 more attend boarding schools. Higher and secondary specialized educational institutions, including correspondence and evening schools, are training 4,450,000 students, of whom 2,400,000 are in higher schools, such as universities and institutes. In addition some 4,970,000 during 1960-61 were receiving part-time training in general, secondary, and higher schools. It has been claimed that 25 per cent of the population are receiving some form of state instruction. Factories and collective farms also maintain night schools for the workers and peasants. The emphasis throughout the educational system is on science, rather than humanities, and on acquiring new skills.

2. The Family

In 1934, there was a return to the concept of the permanency of the family after sixteen years of considering this counter-revolutionary. Divorce at the present time is difficult to obtain. But the family has little time together because of the high degree of "off-time" activities virtually required of all its members if they are to keep in good standing with their superiors and with the party. Children are indoctrinated to report on their parents in school or in the Young Communist Leagues, and in self-protection many parents have erected a wall of silence between themselves and their children on any issue in which a child might innocently divulge parental criticism of the government. The result is a tragic split within the family itself.

3. Medicine

The goal is to make medical services available to everyone. In 1959, when population was 208,826,000, there were 1,618,100 hospital beds and 379,500 doctors. Medical students, after completion of the ten-grade school or its equivalent, pursue a five-year course supplemented by several years of practice. Rural doctors take post-graduate courses every three years. Medical assistants, midwives, nurses, and pharmacy assistants are trained in 985 schools. Private medical treatment is available for those who can afford it. Maternity care is free, and a maternity leave from work is granted the mother. Over half of all children are born in maternity homes. Strong emphasis has been placed on preventive medicine and public health work. This is one phase of Soviet life that seems to be popular with the people.

Voluntary Organizations

In the Soviet there is nothing comparable to voluntary organizations like the Parent-Teachers Association, the Community Chest, and a wide variety of service clubs, veterans' organizations, labor, fraternal, and professional societies, political clubs, and similar groups. The United States, for example, has over six thousand such voluntary groups organized on a national scale but without government supervision of any kind.

Religion

In the years following the Revolution, there was an all-out attempt to destroy religion. The whole power of government propaganda was turned against the churches and some were seized and converted into anti-religious museums. A census taken after twenty years of such efforts is said to have shown that one-half of the Russian people still believed in God. A new constitution adopted about that time (1936) guaranteed freedom of worship and antireligious propaganda, thus implying no freedom for religious propaganda. The Ten Commandments of Communism of the Young Communists League contains the following: "If you are not a convinced atheist, you cannot be a good Communist or a real Soviet citizen. Atheism is indissolubly bound to communism. These two ideals are the pillars of the Soviet Power."

The regime's efforts over nearly half a century to eliminate religion from Russia have been compared with some justification to a struggle for supremacy between old established religions and a new secular religion, represented by the Marxist-Leninist ideology of the Communist Party. According to Communist theory, religion and religious institutions arose with the development of social classes, and they have been traditionally used by "the exploiters to enslave the exploited masses" and to prevent the emergence of revolutionary class consciousness. The regime explains that the continued existence of religious feelings and religious denominations in the "classless" Soviet Union is a "remnant of capitalism" that is to be eradicated.

Some apparent changes in Soviet ways of seeking to accommodate to religion until it can be eradicated and the effect of antireligious communism on the church in the U.S.S.R. will be discussed in the next chapter.

In the Satellites

On the borders of the Soviet Union are the satellite countries of Eastern Europe, so-called because they revolve around the powerful Soviet Union like a small planet revolves around a larger one and to some extent is dependent upon it. The satellites are Albania, Bulgaria, Czechoslovakia, East Germany, Hungary, Poland, and Rumania. Yugoslavia is a Socialist state that maintains a certain independence in its domestic and foreign policies. Poland, close to Russia and dependent upon the U.S.S.R. for her security, seems to be able to carry on a very moderate domestic policy with a very good deal of intellectual freedom. Albania, accused by Khrushchev of favoring "Stalinism" and its practices, was denounced by him at the October, 1961, meetings of the Communist Party of the Soviet Union and defended by Premier Chou En-lai of China.

The Soviet practice in the satellite countries of Eastern Europe, when a full Communist government could not at first be formed, has been to work with a coalition government but to insist upon Communist control of the Ministry of the Interior in order to get control of the police. In a short time the coalition ministers, non-Communists, are pushed out of the government, often on accusations of plotting against the country, and the populace is screened for counterrevolutionaries and "socially dangerous" citizens. "Free and unfettered" elections are held with the help of the police, and a Communist government takes over, usually with personnel trained in Moscow. A new "democratic" constitution is published, land distribution is instituted, the means of production become nationalized, as soon as possible agriculture is collectivized, and an iron curtain falls. The general pattern has been to gear the whole economy of the new satellite into that of the Soviet Union.

As the reins of the Soviet Union are drawn closer, a further stage of screening, accusation, and purging usually follows. In this the more nationalistic elements of the Communist leadership of the country are removed and only those who will follow the lead of Russia are kept in positions of power. This is not easily accomplished. In spite of enthusiastic speeches by delegates to Congress sessions and prolonged applause, there have been signs of unrest in various countries among workers and students and sometimes even among leaders. In 1955, criticism arose in Poland and Hungary, for example. Dissatisfaction with Communist practices was expressed in political rallies and in the press. The uprising in Poland was suppressed after arrests were made by two units of the Soviet-controlled Polish Army and prolonged armed conflict avoided. But in Hungary where defiance began in peaceful demonstrations on the part of students, protests attracted the support of workers and led to a bloody revolution. Appeals for aid to other nations and the United Nations were unanswered. World attention was centered on threats to peace in the Middle East, and the Soviet Army arrived in Hungary within a very brief time and crushed the revolt in bloody fighting. Thousands of Hungarians were killed; many escaped across the Austrian border, and "order" was restored. After this threat to Soviet power in the satellites, screws were loosened then tightened in Poland and East Germany.

Different branches of national and party officials report on each other secretly to Moscow so there are various ways of checking even on high officials. Yugoslavia saw the danger of increasing Russian power before the chance of organizing opposition had been lost. After watching the dominance of Russia gradually grow over his country in unequal economic arrangements, Tito, the Yugoslav leader, with dramatic suddenness stopped the Russian agents who would have controlled his government from the inside. His rebellion constitutes a challenge to the absolute pretension of the Russian interpretation of communism and of Marx; it represents the kind of heresy that strikes at the foundation of international Communist structures and therefore has been reviled fiercely by the Russians.

In the satellite countries, generally, the new government initially tried to win the cooperation of the peasants through land reform, giving most peasants a small plot. As soon as the new government had consolidated its power sufficiently to be able to override the peasants' hostility to the collective farm, an almost complete collectivization was carried out in all these countries except Poland where collectivization still remains a declared objective of the regime. Heavy industry has not been encouraged in satellite countries in order to make them more dependent upon the Soviet Union.

In the People's Republic of China

When the delegates to the Soviet Communist Party met in Moscow October 17, 1961, high-level "fraternal" delegates were present. These visitors came from Asian Communist countries—mainland China, North Korea, Outer Monoglia, and North Vietnam—and other countries in Asia where Communists do not have government control; from Africa and Europe; from North and South America. In some of these countries Communist influence is negligible, in some it is growing, in some it has become a more or less dominant force. Particular attention in press and radio reports was given to China's representatives both because of the strength of the Chinese Communist Party and because of signs of growing differences of point of view between the People's Republic of China and the Union of Soviet Socialist Republics.

The Chinese Communist Party, which controls the daily lives of millions of mainland Chinese, began in a conversation of a small group of men in Shanghai in 1921. Within forty years it grew to have a power that has roused world-wide concern. By the end of World War II in 1945, Communists had a strong position in North China, gained through Soviet influence and training of the leaders, through infiltration into the Nationalist government of China and the weaknesses of that government, and through effective guerilla tactics carried on during the period of war with Japan. By April, 1949, the party was strong enough to occupy the Nationalist's capital at Nanking, and within six months communism spread throughout China with no effective opposition. On October 1, 1949, the People's Republic of China was formally instituted in Peking, with Mao Tse-tung at its head and Chou En-lai as premier.

The appeal of the Chinese Communist Party to the people centered in glowing promises of land reform and a better life for all the Chinese people. Attention was given immediately to the economic plight of the farmers, and party programs moved from the redistribution of land to cooperative procedures and the elimination of private ownership. Next came the setting up of communes, with various adaptations in the approach and methods as successive programs were launched. Reasons why the Chinese people, even many Christians, supported and continue to support the People's Republic of China and work hard toward achieving its goals are summarized as follows by Dr. Francis Price Jones:

> . . . (1) The Communist government has ended the civil war that was ravaging the country and brought peace and stability. (2) It has overcome the ruinous inflation and other economic disorders that had so plagued the country under Nationalist rule. (3) Its positive programs of universal education and health care have appealed to the ethical sense of all, including Christians, and have been a powerful argument on behalf of the Communist claim to care for the common man. (4) There was from the beginning a tremendous patriotic appeal. Communism carefully avoided any appearance of being a foreign ideology and claimed instead to fulfill the legitimate aspirations of all patriotic Chinese. (5) There was no practical alternative to the support of this government. The Nation-

[40]

alist alternative rapidly lost all appeal after the retreat from the mainland, and the only remaining choice was between communism and chaos.[3]

As noted earlier, principles stressed and procedures followed by the Communist Party and government in all countries are much alike. The Chinese Communist Party, the largest such party in the world, has had a high degree of unity of leadership. It has complete control of the military forces in China. Government mandates formulated by top leaders reach every household in the country. Much use has been made of mass organization to educate, to propagandize, and to mobilize all the people to help carry out the party program. New Democratic Youth, the All-China Federation of Democratic Women, and the Sino-Soviet Friendship Association each have millions of enthusiastic members who support the actions and goals of the party and the Chinese People's Republic. Major emphasis is placed upon the ideas and ideals of communism. Dr. A. Doak Barnett, in the report of a 1958 Consultation on China, says:

> It is extraordinary how much attention the Chinese Communists devote not only to what people do but also to what people think. Without doubt ideology is the basic cement which holds together the ruling group and which, to a large degree, explains its unity and its dynamism. But the Chinese Communists appear determined not only to maintain "the faith" within the party itself. They also are attempting to indoctrinate the whole population in the new ideology. Many visitors to both the Soviet Union and Communist China have been struck by the difference between the two countries in this respect. After forty years of bureaucratic ossification, the Soviet leaders do not show the same zeal as the Chinese in attempting to indoctrinate the individual.
>
> In China there is an intense, religious, revivalist flavor about much that the Chinese Communists do. . . . The whole educational system, which has been vastly expanded, and the huge propaganda apparatus, which extends everywhere, hammer new ideas and values into the population constantly. In addition, a large part

[41]

of the population in China, especially in urban groups, is organized into so-called *hsueh hsi* groups, or study groups, to learn by rote a new and unfamiliar version of what is defined to be the truth. In all of this indoctrination the Chinese Communists concern themselves not only with day-to-day matters but also with basic values and attitudes.

It is difficult, of course, to know what the real effect of the indoctrination is upon people's thinking. It is clear that many people, particularly among the older generation, verbally submit to authority while maintaining their own previous views and attitudes privately. There is no question, however, that indoctrination in Communist China is successful in achieving general conformity on the surface, and it seems probable that it is having a great impact upon the values and attitudes of the younger generation in particular. A whole generation is being "molded" with Marxist ideas, with new concepts about the nature of society and history; the criteria for defining "good" and "bad"; the rules which should govern human relations; and the norms governing relations between man and society and man and nature. . . .

In all probability it is the Chinese rather than the Russians who today are the most zealous missionaries for communism in an ideological sense.[4]

In Other Countries

Communist influence is strong in Southeast Asia, and active Communists seek to influence elections and government actions in Japan and India. The U.S.S.R. through propaganda and direct action makes the most of any opportunity to extend the outreach of its power; examples are Cuba, Guinea, Laos, South Vietnam. The People's Republic of China insists that world revolution is inevitable if communism is to triumph. The Chinese Communist Party resists the Soviet Union's emphasis upon the possibility of "peaceful coexistence" with the West and upon means short of war in attaining communism's goals. During and after the Soviet Party's Twenty-second Congress in October, 1961, differences between Soviet and Chinese views became more evident.

[42]

Summary

Assembling a summary of Communist practices may help to reveal how far Communist theory has been carried into constructive action and what some of the results of communism have been in the lives of the people of Communist nations. Points that would merit consideration in such a summary are presented briefly in the following paragraphs.

The people, especially in the Soviet Union, are benefiting in many ways from the educational and social services provided by their Communist state. Illiteracy has been almost abolished in Russia. General culture, although exclusively Marxist, has been brought to the people through the theatre, movies, radio, and schools. Libraries are more numerous. It must be recognized, of course, that all these cultural services are part of the government's method for directing the thinking of the people.

Hospital care and medical services are more widely available to the mass of the people. Life expectancy has increased. Some workers are receiving benefits in the way of vacations at resorts and rest homes.

The Soviet Union has achieved remarkable results in the field of heavy industry, transforming itself in less than fifty years from a comparatively backward power to the world's second greatest industrial producer. Methods of national planning for economic growth have been worked out and developed to a high point. The problems of unemployment have been brought under control by the discipline and manipulation of the workers. The Soviet Union has been in the vanguard in the exploration of outer space and nuclear development.

Less has been accomplished in the field of agriculture, but attempts have been made and are being made through state farms, communes, and other means to produce the food that is needed for the immense population.

Many people have gained a reason for living, new purpose, and direction for their lives as they have worked under communism for a better society. They have been taught that they have a part in the creation of a new society in which everyone will share the good things and that their individual work counts toward an ultimate and worth-while goal.

Much has been accomplished in the U.S.S.R. and other Com-

munist countries, and credit must be given to those who hav
improved conditions. Gains, however, must always be balance
against losses. For example, a sense of brotherhood, based o
involvement in and dedication to a common cause, has deve
oped among Communists around the world, but this brothe
hood is limited to those who accept the central authority of com
munism and is accompanied by a hatred of and opposition to a
non-communist systems. This has created world-wide tensions
Distinctions in the Soviet Union based upon race, it is claimed
have decreased, but Jews have been severely persecuted.

The Communist regime has a disregard for the huma
rights of individuals; the concern has been for the mass. Intrinsic
worth of personality and endeavor directed to the happiness of the
individual person and family have been submerged in efforts on
behalf of the "masses." Memories of the plight of the kulaks and
dissenting leaders and of the fate of the people of Hungary and
Tibet cannot be erased.

There are still shortages in housing, food, and clothing for the
masses after nearly a half century of communism, and this in spite
of remarkable industrial advance. The tendency in economic life
is away from equality in spite of glowing promises for enjoyment of life on the part of all in the future. What was heralded
as a classless society is witnessing the emergence of new classes.

A total political, economic, and social dictatorship by a small
group of official leaders controls and directs the lives and affairs
of 200 million Soviet citizens and many other millions in the
satellites and other countries. Such dictatorship, which is expressed in different ways country by country, has spread to
China and other parts of Asia and is moving into Africa and
Latin America. The people under communism have no freedom
to oppose party policies or to criticize the existing government.
They know only what they are told by the party, and the ten-
tacles of the secret police reach out into every factory, farm,
home, school, and office, sowing tension, distrust, and suspicion.

Communists labor diligently to remove all references to or
consciousness of God and to make themselves the final arbiters in
matters of human destiny. "The end justifies the means," it is
claimed, and the end is the success of the revolution whatever the
cost may be in human life or character. There is no recognition
of Divine Justice above the little efforts of men.

The Communist Party of the Soviet Union with all its national branches is dedicated to world conquest often camouflaged under the banner of peace. Stalin once said: "For what else is our country, the country that is building socialism, if not the base of world revolution?"

The Soviet Union, the nation that has preached most strongly against colonialism, shows the greatest determination and exhibits the most ability to subjugate other nations. At the end of the last war, Russia annexed greater areas of land than any other country. Now Soviet power is being extended over an ever-widening system of satellite controls. The peoples brought under Communist influence are incorporated into a tightly integrated system the centers of which are Moscow and Peking.

In all this a fine distinction is drawn between the "authority of leader," like Premier Khrushchev, and the dictatorship and excesses of Stalin, termed "the cult of personality." In a speech at the Twenty-Second Congress, the head of the Department of Agitation and Propaganda of the Communist Party's Central Committee said:

> The party does its utmost to exclude the possibility of a revival of the cult of personality. But it does and will do everything to protect the authority of its leaders, who are dedicating all their energies to the people, to the cause of the triumph of communism.[5]

Communism comes preaching world brotherhood but practising a new type of imperialism growing out of the dream of world revolution, an imperialism that not only resorts to military conquest but is not satisfied until it imposes its absolute control over the minds and hearts of men. It is in effect a Soviet colonialism.

Dr. Charles Malik, former President of the United Nations and a Greek Orthodox layman, in an address to the Second National Conference of Southern Baptist Men, at Memphis, Tennessee, sums up communism in theory and practice in these words:

> The character of the Communist challenge consists, first, in a conception of matter, man, society, history, government, and the supreme being radically differ-

ent from and opposite to anything you and I and o
ancestors have known for the last four thousand year
second, in the existence of a superbly organized polit
cal party with an absolutely dedicated membership a
over the world . . . actively working to bring ever
people on earth under the bondage of this philosoph
. . . third, in this party's use of every conceivabl
means—war, revolution, subversion, infiltration, prop
aganda, intimidation, dictatorship, manipulation of th
masses, smear tactics, character assassination, excitin
the basest instincts in man, playing up differences an
grievances between nations and peoples and races an
classes—to attain its unalterable ends of world domi
nation; fourth, in the fact that this world revolutionary
thrust is backed by one of the most powerful military
establishments in the world . . . and fifth, in the fac
that this world revolutionary force . . . has succeeded
in extending and consolidating its iron hold upon a
least a third of the human race. . . . [6]

The Church and Communism

Chapter 4

ommunism has gained power in many countries where there are hristian churches, but many Christian people still do not understand the Communist policy toward the church. One reason for is lack of understanding is that Communist governments have fferent and changing policies.

Religious Freedom

Many things appear to indicate that Communist governments ve full religious freedom to Christians. Practically all of the ommunist countries guarantee freedom of worship in their nstitutions. Seldom today are Christians being prosecuted rectly for their religious faith. Churchmen are tried, but it is for imes that they are said to have committed, not for the faith ey hold.

When a Communist government comes to power, it gives broad surances to the people of their rights and liberties, not the ast of these being religious liberty. For example, as the Chinese ommunist Army advanced, their agents put up posters on urches in each newly conquered area assuring the people of ligious freedom. In North Korea a Russian commander is own to have visited the pastor in Wonsan and urged him to rry on with his Christian activities as usual.

Such incidents suggest that communism gives full freedom to e church. Yet they are only part of the story. Assurances given hen a government first comes to power may be only a clever ethod for allaying opposition and keeping people quiet until power can be consolidated. Other factors indicate that the Communist policy is to destroy the church, root and branch, using every power the state can exercise.

There are numerous examples that show how this type of policy has been carried out. In the early years in Russia when Communist revolutionaries first took power, they killed priests in many places and closed churches in large numbers. In North Korea after the beginning of the war in 1950, there were wholesale arrests and executions of Christian ministers. Hundreds were thrown into jail and later marched off into the hills and shot. Not only ministers were thus attacked, but other trained Christian leaders, both laymen and women, were treated in the same way. In some areas 60 to 80 per cent of the Christian leaders were killed.

The Soviets' avowed intention was to eliminate religion and religious "remnants" from the Soviet Union, thus preventing religious denominations from playing an active role in formulating Soviet values and cultural patterns. But stability, nationalism, and obedience to authority, which the Russian Orthodox Church over the years had endorsed among believers, have apparently led the Communists at times of great danger—such as during World War II—to call upon the church for its support.

Three Important Points

In addition to what has been said about the Communist attitude toward religion and the church, three points that very largely determine the Communist attitude toward the church must be considered further. These points are the Communist understanding of religion, the demands of the totalitarian state, and the principle of democratic centralism.

Communist Understanding of Religion

Communism insists that religious belief is a result of the imperfect state of human knowledge of world, man, and society. As science progresses and ignorance decreases, religious superstition will die out. The Communists consider religion as a product of the class structure of society. It is because different classes exist with one class oppressing another, they claim, that man needs religion. The purpose of religion is only to keep people who are oppressed and exploited contented with their lot, looking forward

[48]

to happiness in the next world rather than demanding justice and happiness on this earth.

Religion, teaches the Communist, merely assures wealthy people that their blessings come from God and so they need not worry about their exploitation of their fellowmen. Lenin meant all this when he wrote:

> Religion teaches those who toil in poverty all their lives to be resigned and patient in this world and consoles them with the hope of reward in heaven. As for those who live upon the labour of others, religion teaches them to be charitable in earthly life, thus providing a cheap justification for their whole exploiting existence and selling them at reasonable price tickets to heavenly bliss. Religion is the opium of the people. Religion is a kind of spiritual intoxicant, in which the slaves of capital drown their humanity and their desires for some sort of decent human existence.[1]

Lenin also declared:

> The Communist Party of the Soviet Union is guided by the conviction that only the conscious and deliberate planning of the social and economic activities of the masses will cause religious prejudice to die out. The Party . . . facilitates the real emancipation of the working masses from religious prejudices and organizes the widest possible scientific, educational, and anti-religious propaganda. At the same time it is necessary carefully to avoid giving such offense to the religious sentiments of believers as only leads to the strengthening of religious fanaticism.[2]

That Khrushchev wholly agrees with Lenin is evident in his 1955 statement during a visit of French notables to Moscow. He said:

> Communism has not changed its attitude of opposition to religion. We are doing everything we can to eliminate the bewitching power of the opium of religion.[3]

And on another occasion, Khrushchev declared:

[49]

> I think there is no God. I freed myself long ago from
> such a concept. I am a partisan of a scientific point of
> view, and science and faith in supernatural forces are
> irreconcilable opinions which exclude one another nec-
> essarily if one is consistent to the end in scientific
> opinions.[4]

No truly committed Communist would favor or accept any
kind of religion, even one that taught people to set the world
right rather than to be content to live under evil conditions. In
fact Lenin thought that the more refined a religion, the more it
covers up the fact that it is an opium and the more harmful it becomes, because it is more difficult for the believing workers to
understand its true reactionary role.

In brief, a classless society has no need or place for religious
belief. When communism establishes its perfect society, it is
assumed that people will forget all about religion and churches
will naturally disappear.

Demands of the Totalitarian State

The second point determining Communist attitude toward the
church arises out of the demands of the totalitarian state. The
Communist state, since it is totalitarian, can brook no competi-
tive allegiance. There can be no independent elements in society.
Everything must be within the total structure of state controls.
There is no place for free trade unions, free business power, or
any other center of power or allegiance that might be separate
from the state. All must be absorbed or "domesticated." All this
holds true just as much for the church as for any other organization or center of allegiance in a Communist society. This is why
Christians are not chosen for positions of responsibility in the
government of the U.S.S.R.

Principle of Democratic Centralism

The third point is what the Communists call the principle of
"democratic centralism," which indicates the method by which all
principles are to be applied. Though decisions in a Communist
country are to be made at the center by those in authority in the
government, men who are also party leaders, there is to be "democratic" participation by all the people in those decisions. At this
point communism is not like the tyrannies of old in which the

tyrant simply made decisions for the whole country and otherwise left men alone. In the new tyranny everyone must be involved in everything that the government decides; constant participation is required. So ways to accomplish this must be devised.

One example is the way in which Communist governments stir up mass fury against the people whom they have decided to execute. The following quotation from a Chinese Communist newspaper shows how a Christian gathering was used to stir up hatred against a well-known evangelist on a trumped-up charge:

> Already our police have arrested the American spy, Ku Jen-en. All the delegates from the four cities of Tsingtao, Shanghai, Hangchow, and Tientsin—Wang Chung-shen, Wang Chihkun, Z. S. Zia, Niu Chih-fang and Ch'iao Wei-hsiu—spat when they angrily reported how he spied in most of those four places. Then the executive chairman of the conference, Y. T. Wu, read from the People's paper of that day (20th) a letter from Yang Shao-Peng, accusing Ku Jen-en of raping his daughter six years ago. As a result the daughter went crazy and to this day is bedridden. He is an "injure heaven and harm reason" rotten Christian. This aroused the whole body of delegates to anger, and when Wang Chung-shen rushed to the platform and fiercely asked, "Does Ku Jen-en deserve death or does he not?" everyone at once roared in anger, "He ought to die! He ought to die!"

A Policy Toward Religion

If we take these three points in combination, they indicate a policy toward religion and the church that might be defined thus: Religion will inevitably disappear. Therefore, all-out efforts to destroy it are not necessary and are not desirable; they only increase the fanaticisim of its followers. Accordingly, it is best to make religion, while it exists, the servant of the totalitarian state, providing constant mass participation in all government programs. A study of the actions of Communist governments shows that this policy not only agrees with basic Communist theory. It also agrees with actual Communist practice.

[51]

E. Louise Patten Library
Piedmont College
Demorest, Georgia   30535

Communism and the Church

Turning from theory to practice, the Communist government has a series of steps it takes with regard to the church, steps that do not come in a certain order but are practically universal in Communist states.

Nationalization of Lands and Institutions

This includes the seizing of all church lands by the government, and it is here that the fight between communism and the Roman Catholic Church usually develops first.

Nationalization of Education

This is extremely important for the Communists because they have an extensive program of education they want to substitute for any system of religious education. Not only does a Communist government close all church schools, it also makes an effort to keep young people away from the extra-curricular activities of the church. Parades are often held at Sunday school time. Communist youth groups are organized in competition with Christian youth societies, and advancement in school or college for young people often depends upon their willingness to join the Communist organization. Theological seminaries are usually the one division of Christian education the church is allowed to operate, but textbooks used are normally censored and the teachings of Marxian doctrine is required. While tolerating religion, Communists are destroying it through education.

Nationalization of Social Services

Medical work, social settlement work, playgrounds, rural development work, cooperative societies, and libraries and reading rooms are early taken away from church bodies and put under agents of the government. Christians have often thought that such social services would be one side of church activity that Communists would welcome and permit. Yet almost universally social services have been the first activities that the Communists have forbidden the church to continue.

The result is that the church is confined to formal services of worship in the church, with set prayers and hymns, icons, candles, incense, and colorful vestments. This accords with the Communist understanding of religion, for if the church can be cut off from all contact with practical life, Communists believe it will more rapidly wither away.

Restriction of Church Activities

The church is allowed to carry on no activities outside its own buildings for such activity might attract public attention. The Russian law has provided that churches should have no organizations for women, children, or youth, no meetings for study or teaching, and no social events or other such gatherings. Any teaching about Christianity has to be on an informal basis and at no regular time. In Communist lands outside of Russia and China, restrictions have not gone this far. Christian organizations still exist in satellite countries, but the tendency of Communists is to weaken their influence.

Active Antireligious Propaganda

This propaganda varies greatly in intensity from period to period and country to country, and a variety of approaches in addition to education are used. The "League of Militant Godless," disbanded in 1941, was revived in 1957 after an atheistic conference held in Moscow by the Communist Party of the Soviet Union. Also in 1957, the government established at Odessa the "House of the Atheist," the first institution devoted exclusively to atheistic indoctrination and training. Since then other universities and schools have been established to indoctrinate youth with an atheistic view of life. Furthermore, youth organizations are encouraged to engage as widely as possible in antireligious campaigns and rallies.

More important than the extent of the antireligious propaganda is the fact that religious propaganda is severely restricted. The Russian church is permitted to publish only one magazine and this must be largely given over to official statements and information. Publication and distribution of the Bible is restricted but is still going on to some extent. In 1926, the All Russian Evangelical Christian Union published an edition of the Bible from plates made at the expense of the American Bible Society, and an edition of the New Testament and Psalms was similarly printed in 1927. One edition of the New Testament and Psalms was printed in 1934 at the expense of the Russian Bible Fund, and a Bible was printed in Warsaw in 1939. In 1956, a large Bible was published in Moscow by the Synod of the Russian

Church and also a New Testament and Psalms, the first Bibles printed by the Synod since 1917. In 1957, ten thousand Bibles were printed in Moscow by the All Union Council of Evangelical Christian Baptists in Russia from plates made from matrices sent by the American Bible Society. Parcel-post and freight shipments of Bibles are not admitted to the U.S.S.R. but some copies are taken in by travelers. Some visitors, however, report difficulties with custom officers when Bibles were found in their luggage.

Scriptures are still printed in Poland, Hungary, and East Germany, and a number of editions were printed in Czechoslovakia up to 1957. In 1956, a delegation of Australian Anglicans visited China and reported that the China Bible House in Shanghai had in the period from 1949 to 1954 distributed more Chinese Scriptures than the American Bible Society had distributed among overseas Chinese in the same period.

Only one Christian magazine is still being published in China, *Tien Feng*, the organ of the Three-Self Movement, and this publication is completely subservient to the Communist line.

Spying in Churches

This is a general practice in all Communist countries. North Korean pastors have reported that at times the "visitors" in their congregations exceeded the actual members of the church who were in attendance. In addition to spies from the outside, members of the congregation are often led to be informers who report what the others are thinking and saying. The result is that mutual trust within a group of Christians is destroyed, and fear and uncertainty are substituted for confidence in one another.

Elimination of Church Leaders Unwilling to Conform

This is never done on religious charges, for the Communists know the propaganda value of martyrdom, but on charges of lawbreaking as indicated earlier in this chapter. The process for such elimination of leaders is standardized. Arrests are usually made at night and followed by several months of confinement when the prisoner is unheard from. Then comes a trial with full confession of the charges that have been made against him, and this is followed by a severe sentence.

It is the confessions of outstanding church leaders that have caused the greatest amazement. Why do men who have been models of integrity confess to crimes they never committed? The clue to the answer to this question is in the months of silence that follow the arrest. During that period the man is completely cut off from the world outside. He has no idea of the date, the week, the month, or even whether it is day or night. He is not allowed to receive any information about anyone who has been acquainted with him. He is not permitted to have reading matter or anything else that might take his attention from himself. He is subjected to endless hours of questioning during which he is kept standing. The questioning often comes during the middle of the night, and he is purposely kept very tired through the question period. There is a constant dinning of the same ideas into his head. Under these conditions the man becomes weary and confused, gives in a little here and there, and begins to lose his bearings; he cannot think for himself and begins to accept suggestions.

When a man has reached this condition, the questioners begin the process of "grafting ideas." The Communists have made a long and thorough investigation of his life and on this basis they present a new interpretation to him of the things that he has done. They confuse unimportant happenings and change little details, giving past acts a different color. This process of "brainwashing" is continued for months. Sometimes extreme physical torture is added, especially if investigation shows a person is weakened rather than strengthened by pain. At last the man is ready to confess to the crimes of which he has been accused. One of the most flagrant examples of such treatment in China is the story of the evangelist Wang Ming-tao who after one year in prison came out completely broken in mind and spirit.

Severance of All Church Ties with Other Lands

The stopping of all mission work in China is the best known example of this, but it is a common practice in all other Communist countries. The lesson all Christian churches must learn is that they have to be able to stand on their own feet. Through tithing and other means they must be able to support themselves and not depend for their existence upon the Christians of other lands. Even correspondence and informal contacts with Christians in non-Communist countries can become so dangerous that the church has to stop them. Very few contacts are allowed even between churches that are in different Communist countries.

These various steps on the part of the state and the party are for all practical purposes one. The church must serve the state. There are endless petitions to circulate, campaigns to take part in, programs to support and promote. In situation after situation, the right of the state and the right of the church must be determined. Churchmen are continually facing uncertainty about how far the church should go.

The Church Today in the Soviet Union

While precise figures are lacking, an estimate of the total number of the adherents of faiths in the Soviet Union today is between one-fourth and one-third of the present population. At the same time all available evidence leads to the conclusion that the importance of religious observances is diminishing. The total number of stated adherents of all denominations has dropped from approximately 80 per cent of the 1917 population to approximately 25 to 35 per cent of the 1960 population. However, most recent visitors to the Soviet Union report that the few places of worship open in cities are crowded. What is not known is the degree to which religiously inclined people refuse or hesitate to practice their religion because of possible ridicule or harassment from the government.

Available information indicates that older people predominate among churchgoers, with elderly women constituting the majority of the worshipers. The rural population is probably more inclined toward religious belief than urban dwellers. There is some evidence that most of the intellectuals and white-collar workers have become irreligious.

Soviet sources complain about youth, even including Young Communist League members, who attend services regularly or occasionally. Generally Soviet press accounts indicate that young people attending churches do so out of curiosity, boredom, or desire to sanctify their marriage. The Young Communist League is urged to combat these tendencies by making their own activities more attractive.

While the importance of religion to the people as a whole appears to be waning, there are groups to whom religious customs and rites are still important. The Soviet press mentions with unconcealed irritation instances of work stoppages, particularly in rural areas, because citizens are celebrating a religious holiday.

Such holidays frequently coincide with the harvest season, and the press complains that harvesting is delayed for several days while revelries continue.

Despite persecution and basic doctrinal conflicts with the government, there appears to be little doubt that in the event of a test of national unity and stability, the major religious denominations in the Soviet Union would be loyal to the Communist regime.

The Soviet government checks on church activities down to the regional level. All appointments to the hierarchies of the various denominations are subject to governmental approval. In the case of the Roman Catholic Church, the regime has allowed, with Vatican approval, some promotions in direct contrast to earlier policy. Any small concession on the part of the government is pointed to as an example of religious toleration on the part of the state and provides propaganda material.

The Church in China

In China, communism decreased the membership of the Chinese Protestant churches from about 1,000,000 in 1949 to not more than 600,000 in 1951. Since then the number has been going up slowly due to new baptisms and returning penitents. Although there is no positive evidence that any church leader has been put to death, communism has removed from office leaders critical of the Communist regime so that the church in China is a thoroughly captive church.

Communists have decreased church activities greatly, not by any antichurch campaign but by so regimenting the time of all Chinese, Christians and non-Christians, so that they have no time for anything beyond working, attending Communist lectures, eating, and sleeping.

Both Protestant and Roman Catholic Christians are recognized by the government and have their officially elected deputies in the peoples' congresses of the government at all levels—village, county, provincial, and national. On one occasion the Reverend Marcus Cheng, a member of the Shanghai Municipal Congress, told that body that the right of antireligious propaganda granted to Communists gave them the right to use whatever rational arguments they could adduce against religion, but it did not give them the right to mock or ridicule the sacred be-

liefs of any of their fellow citizens and that those who did so
were guilty of a crime as great as that of defiling the tombs of
one's ancestors.

In China the Communists have molded Christian teaching
into a pattern as nearly as possible like Communist teachings.
They have allowed Christians to teach the existence of God, but
he must be a God who looks with approval upon the Communist
program.

The Church in the Satellites

Over the past decade news has come from Communist countries in Eastern Europe indicating that Christians are struggling
to give their witness in difficult times. From Hungary news tells
of a new life movement throughout the church with churches
packed. One church with a membership of over five thousand
reported 461 Bible study circles.

From East Germany come reports that laymen are awaking to
their church responsibility.

A letter from Czechoslovakia brings the message:

> Rougher classes are taking over the direction of so-
> ciety. From the human point of view the present sit-
> uation is much more painful for the church. All outside
> support has been withdrawn. And yet from the point
> of view of the Church of Christ, we are on the thresh-
> old of a finer and more blessed age. In the future we
> shall not be able to depend upon anything at all—
> neither upon wealth, nor upon homage paid to us by
> society, nor upon any human aid, but solely upon the
> grace and love of God.

According to a news report from Berlin in the fall of 1961, the
unity of the German church has been preserved so far despite
the closing of the border. Some Communist attempts to split
the German Evangelical Church were disclosed, but so far the
Council of German Evangelical Churches in Germany, the
church's steering body with headquarters in West Berlin, has
been able to co-ordinate activities in both parts of the country
through daily personal contacts. Details concerning these contacts could not be given for security reasons.

The Communist Party chief in Poland, Wladyslaw Gomulka,

asserted recently that his party has a long struggle ahead against religious belief in Poland. In a rare interview, he said:

> Religion is deeply rooted in a major part of our population. It is difficult to say how long religious belief will persist in Poland—certainly for tens of years and possibly even longer.[5]

Controversy had flared over the question of religious instruction eliminated from Polish public schools by government decree in 1960.

Religious instruction was transferred to "catechism" points in church buildings, parish halls, and priests' quarters. The government then ordered priests to register these catechism points, but the church told the priests to defy the order.

Evidence that church life continues in Eastern Europe is found in a bulletin titled "Current Developments in the Eastern European Churches" issued by the Desk for Documentation concerning Eastern European Churches of the World Council of Churches in Geneva. The introduction to the August, 1961, issue calls the reader's attention to its reports of what is going on in the religious and antireligious life in Eastern European countries where "side by side with a strong and powerful Christian conception of life there is a conception of life proudly based on what is called atheistic morality . . . one of the most striking intellectual and spiritual developments in the life of mankind today."

This issue of the bulletin tells of a journey made by His Holiness Patriarch Alexius of Moscow to the heads of the ancient churches in Constantinople, the Near East, Greece, and Egypt "to promote unity and friendship between the churches." Cordial and fraternal meetings were reported and exchange of news of church life. The consecration of the thirty-two year-old Archbishop of Yaroslav and Rostov and his journey with a young Baptist interpreter to the enthronement of the 100th Archbishop of Canterbury were also reported.

In the same bulletin it was stated that the year's budget in Czechoslovakia included an item for restoration and repair of churches and that the Hungarian Ecumenical Council sent greetings to Dr. Karl Barth on his seventy-fifth birthday with glowing tribute to his work and prayers for God's blessing upon him.

Representatives of the Lutheran World Federation Executive Committee, meeting in Warsaw in June, 1961, urged the members of their churches "to continue to carry out with courage and patience the task of the Church of Jesus Christ in the world, so that the fear of God may rule the nations, and that true peace may reign and that genuine reconciliation may bring about real fellowship of all men."

Deepening of the Christian Faith

In and through all the church life and the difficulties Christians are facing in Communist nations, a deepening and intensification of faith is evident, which gives church membership new meaning. There are no impressive large-scale advances, but individuals and small groups are coming together with a deeper understanding of what Christianity means in their lives. They may have no Bible schools, no church clubs or youth groups, no church recreational halls, no orphanages or hospitals, no endowments or estates, and no church papers. They often have no set hours or places for worship. The pastors live in simple bare quarters along with their parishioners. Yet there is evidence that the church remains a living, worshiping community, holding life in common and exercising a ministry of evangelism and of mutual comfort and encouragement and converting many of those whose lives they touch.

Some people feel that though this deepening of personal religion is good as far as it goes, it is inevitably stunted and inadequate because it has to be removed from national life and politics and the church can give no social witness. But is not this doing an injustice to Christians under communism? Every act, even the simplest, now involves for them responsible decisions for society. Everything has political significance. Politics begins as soon as one steps outside the church door. The quality of Christian life itself has political importance, and it stands as a rebuke to many political demands and political stands. In showing love for all and trying to bring Christ to all, the church is witnessing before communism. Who knows but that it is witnessing in the way that will in the long run prove most effective? A pastor in Hungary when asked "What are you doing about communism?" replied, "Nothing but preach Christ." But could any man anywhere do more?

| Chapter 5 | The Christian Way |

The Christian's basic source book is the Holy Bible. Here he finds thoughts and experiences of men and women that reflect the encounter between God and the human race over many generations. Here he reads the gospel of Jesus of Nazareth and sees the relation of Jesus Christ to God as Son and to man as Lord and Savior. Through Bible study, the Christian becomes acquainted with events and discoveries during the early days of the Christian church and sees how the followers of Jesus became the embodiment of the way of salvation he had proclaimed. Today millions of Christians in every nation on earth look back to those early days of Christianity in the light of the accumulated experience of twenty centuries and gain insights for their own lives.

Some Basic Insights

Both the Old Testament and the New help the Christian to understand the nature and purpose of God. "In the beginning God created the heavens and the earth" (Genesis 1:1). This early insight of man is basic to Christian faith and understanding. The Christian knows and firmly believes that at the center of the universe, as Creator and Sustainer, is the Eternal God, the Father of the Lord Jesus Christ. The assurance that relationship to God is part of every human experience and that God is the overruling judge of every nation and the ever-present help of every person in time of trouble has led Christians of every generation to face danger triumphantly.

Awareness of the nature of God has been a growing concept in human experience. Long ago the Psalmist declared:

> The heavens are telling the glory of God;
> and the firmament proclaims his handiwork.
> Day to day pours forth speech,
> and night to night declares knowledge.
>
> PSALMS 19:1-2

Modern scientists testify to the rule of law and order and purpose in the universe that the Psalms reflect. Albert Einstein, the world-famed German-born physicist, is said to have remarked that one day man will prove what now he hardly dares surmise, that electro-magnetism, atomic radiation, and the love of God are all parts of one whole reality.

The Christian discovers in the person of Jesus Christ other vivid insights into the nature and purpose of God. He is the Word made flesh; he is in himself a divine communication, revealing the power and goodness of God. The meaning of the Christian faith is rooted in the incarnation of Christ, the cross, and the resurrection. Its meaning is clearly set forth for all time by St. Paul:

> Have this mind among yourselves, which you have
> in Christ Jesus, who, though he was in the form of
> God, did not count equality with God a thing to be
> grasped, but emptied himself, taking the form of a
> servant, being born in the likeness of men. And being
> found in human form he humbled himself and
> became obedient unto death, even death on a cross.
> Therefore God has highly exalted him and bestowed
> on him the name which is above every name, that at
> the name of Jesus every knee should bow, in heaven
> and on earth and under the earth, and every tongue
> confess that Jesus Christ is Lord, to the glory of God
> the Father.   PHILIPPIANS 2:5-11

All who have bowed in allegiance to Christ, all who over twenty centuries have confessed him as Lord, comprise his Universal Church. As God revealed himself through the person of Jesus Christ, so through the centuries he has used the church to the limit of its obedience to publish divine good news. This good news is summarized in St. John's words:

> For God so loved the world that he gave his only Son, that whoever believes in him should not perish but have eternal life.
> JOHN 3:16

In succeeding verses John points out that God's love is addressed to the world in order to save it. To all who rebel against the rule of God and the Lordship of Christ, a clear judgment is stated:

> ... the light has come into the world, and men loved darkness rather than light, because their deeds were evil.
> JOHN 3:19

To the Christian church today Paul proclaims the same truth, declaring that God has made ample provision through Christ for reconciling the entire world to his loving rule:

> He destined us in love to be his sons through Jesus Christ, according to the purpose of his will, to the praise of his glorious grace which he freely bestowed on us in the Beloved. In him we have redemption through his blood, the forgiveness of our trespasses, according to the riches of his grace which he lavished upon us. For he has made known to us in all wisdom and insight the mystery of his will, according to his purpose which he set forth in Christ as a plan for the fullness of time, to unite all things in him, things in heaven and things on earth.
> EPHESIANS 1:5-10

This Church, the body of Christ, is one in the sense that all believers acknowledge and confess one Lord; the gospel of the Good News of Christ is undivided. And just as Christ considered himself a servant, so his church is servant of all with many ministries to perform. The church is one in spirit and purpose, yet the form of organization and expression among Christian believers is as varied as the shapes of the leaves in the forest. Herein lie freedom, variety, and full play for individual and group initiative. The divine dynamic of the Holy Spirit, as free as the wind, is the generating power within and alongside the church.

[63]

What Is the Church?

Although many statements have been made about its nature and purpose and history, the church itself still remains undefined. It may be called the reign of God's redeeming grace; as such it finds expression in a given generation by reacting in a special way to its peculiar needs. After the Roman Empire crumbled, for example, the church became a fortress of Christian truth and ancient learning, rendering its appropriate form of service for that date.

The church may be called the power of Christ's hidden Kingship. In response to critical challenge, it bursts out quite unpredictably into new energy. The Protestant Reformation was such a phenomenon, as is the ecumenical movement of the twentieth century.

The church may also appropriately be called the working of the Holy Spirit for, through ancient channels and new and effective ones, the Holy Spirit is ever bringing the church fresh power. This perennial renewal of the church by the Holy Spirit is truly a mystery and continuing proof that it is a chosen tool in the hand of God shaped to serve his purpose. The many forms of the church have all been blessed by this renewing power, forms that are strictly hierarchical and forms that maintain the universal priesthood of all believers, forms known as established churches and those that call themselves "free."

Christlike Living

Christians see in Jesus Christ the fulfillment of the ideal of the Suffering Servant described by Isaiah:

> Surely he has borne our griefs
>   and carried our sorrows;
> yet we esteemed him stricken,
>   smitten by God, and afflicted.
> But he was wounded for our transgressions,
>   he was bruised for our iniquities;
> upon him was the chastisement that made us whole,
>   and with his stripes we are healed.

ISAIAH 53:4-5

Jesus spoke of himself as a servant and told his disciples to devote themselves to the redemptive service of God:

[64]

> . . . You know that the rulers of the Gentiles lord
> it over them, and their great men exercise authority
> over them. It shall not be so among you; but whoever
> would be great among you must be your servant, and
> whoever would be first among you must be your
> slave; even as the Son of man came not to be served
> but to serve, and to give his life as a ransom for many.
>
> MATTHEW 20:25-27

This way of life has never been a popular one, especially during periods when proud and ruthless tyrants have murdered those who opposed them and regimented the masses. But the Christian finds his basic motivation in the divine humility of his Lord who washed his disciples' feet. In his name the Christian offers obedient service to God, approaching the deepest needs of men and nations with redemptive concern and service designed to liberate rather than to dominate. In such a spirit, the Christian finds perfect freedom. When total allegiance is given to one Lord, the threats of earthly dictators lose their power.

Jesus Christ was in himself the Word, and the words that he spoke, as recorded in the New Testament, are the gospel to which Christians turn today for guidance. This gospel tells who Christ was and what he did and said. It reveals his mission to mankind. It makes it clear that his church is in itself a mission and also that it has many missions. The command that he gave to his followers empowers Christians and directs them to corporate witness:

> . . . All authority in heaven and earth have been given
> to me. Go therefore and make disciples of all nations,
> baptizing them in the name of the Father and of the
> Son and of the Holy Spirit, teaching them to observe all
> that I have commanded you; and lo, I am with you
> always, to the close of the age.   MATTHEW 28:18-20

In obedience to this command, witnesses have fanned out from the small country of Palestine into every nation on earth. Today millions of Christians are witnessing for Christ on every frontier, working on both sides of every curtain or other artificial barrier disrupting the fellowship of man.

The commission's verbs—*go, make* [disciples], *baptize,* and *teach*—have been obeyed in myriad forms across the years as Christians have sought to be effective witnesses in their encounter with society. A tireless evangelistic thrust has made the Christian faith known; the <u>Bible</u>, as a whole or in part, has been printed in <u>1,165 languages.</u> The gospel is being communicated today in spoken word and by printed page, through filmstrips, motion pictures, radio, and television. The teaching mission of the church has nurtured every form of education. Doctors and nurses have carried forward a varied health ministry. The church is in the forefront of the effort to banish illiteracy and to provide the inspiration and skills for producing indigenous Christian literature. At all these and other points, the church is zealously engaged in the battle for the primary loyalty of man to Christ.

The relevance of the Christian faith for the twentieth century becomes apparent when one considers the condition of society at points opposed to Christian principles. As indicated earlier in this book, careful observers of secular society point out that for vast numbers life has lost all meaning and lasting enjoyment. Where there is no faith, life is a round of meaningless activities. Men are born, know a few brief moments of excitement, suffer senselessly, and die without dignity. When life becomes a constantly narrowing spiral, it ends with ingrown personality clutching its last possession—despair. The church today in new ways addresses its gospel to the secular, materialistic fraction of mankind—to those with no higher goal in life than increased production and a comfortable standard of living.

Christianity Versus Communism

Christianity relates man to God. Communism cuts man off from any god at all, from anything spiritual or transcendent. It laughs at the idea of anything real apart from the material world in which man lives today. It belittles Christian worship and forbids Christian teaching of youth.

Christianity relates man to God. Communism takes man, puts him at the center of life's stage, and focuses all attention on him. The Communist's world is the one he lives in here and now, a world of science with science as the sole guide to a full life. There is no other world for man, present or future.

The practice of this atheism, this godlessness of communism

as certain consequences. It means that man stands alone with no Judge before whom he will be called to account for his actions. The Communist has no God and, therefore, no conscience to respond to an inner divine voice and no divine law as his basic universal code of morality and human decency.

The drift of this modern age of technology increasingly leads more and more people to believe that science alone can solve their problems. The Communists glorify science, set it up as an idol, and operate behind it. To exalt science to this degree implies that human reason alone is keen enough to discover all that can be known about life. Anyone who believes that this is possible is saying that man by himself can learn all there is to know about this world, that only man really matters, that no God is needed.

Jesus Christ said, "I am the way, the truth, and the life," but to the atheistic Communist, truth is revealed not by God through Christ but by the Kremlin in Moscow and in what the party says the faithful must believe. Trotsky, who was one of the chief leaders of the Russian Revolution but later put out of the party and murdered, wrote in 1924:

> The party in the last analysis is always right because the party is the single historic instrument given to the proletariat for the solution of its fundamental problems. . . . I know that one must not be right against the party, one can be right only with the party, and through the party, for history has created no other road for the realization of what is right.[1]

In a Communist country only one opinion counts, that of the party. Not only is there no freedom in opposition to the government, there is not even the freedom of silence. Any individual who is not loud enough in his praise of the party is looked upon with suspicion.

The Individual and the Mass

The Christian teaching is that every human being has infinite worth for:

> Are not two sparrows sold for a penny? And not one of them will fall to the ground without your Father's will. But even the hairs of your head are all numbered.

> Fear not, therefore; you are of more value than many
> sparrows. MATTHEW 10:29-31

Christianity teaches that all men should love one another and serve one another, for all are bound individually to God and so all are bound to one another. In his letter to the Romans, Paul wrote:

> Live in harmony with one another; do not be haughty,
> but associate with the lowly; never be conceited. Re-
> pay no one evil for evil, but take thought for what is
> noble in the sight of all. If possible, so far as it depends
> upon you, live peaceably with all. . . . Do not be
> overcome by evil, but overcome evil with good.
> ROMANS 12:16-18; 21

To the Communist, humanity in the mass is all that is important, because he has no God before whom the individual takes on meaning as a single soul. What really matters is the common or collective good of society. Every person must therefore, willingly or unwillingly, subordinate himself to the common good.

At the time of the 1917 Russian Revolution, workers were told that they must ruthlessly crush their enemies, the bourgeoisie. Enemies, according to Communists, are those who stand in the way of the progress of society. Therefore they must be liquidated, done away with in the most complete and drastic way possible. All who stand in the way of the party are "enemies of the people," no matter what services they may have rendered in the past, no matter if they have been prominent leaders of the party itself. No man has personal rights, no common humanity to which to appeal.

It is this denial by Communists of the basic worth of persons created by God that permits them to do frightful things and to call those deeds right. Impersonal cruelty in dealing with "enemies," which has shocked the rest of the world, is ethical according to Communist theory and hence practised.

In centering attention on man alone, rather than on man in relation to God, the system loses sight of the worth of the person as an individual and so is radically at odds with the Christian faith.

[68]

The Reality of Sin

Jesus taught that sin has its roots fixed deep in every human heart. Paul wrote to the Christians at Rome:

> I do not understand my own actions. For I do not do what I want, but I do the very thing I hate. Now if I do what I do not want, I agree that the law is good. So then it is no longer I that do it, but sin which dwells within me. For I know that nothing good dwells within me, that is, in my flesh. I can will what is right, but I cannot do it. For I do not do the good I want, but the evil I do not want is what I do. . . . So I find it to be a law that when I want to do right evil lies close at hand. For I delight in the law of God, in my inmost self, but I see in my members another law at war with the law of my mind and making me captive to the law of sin which dwells in my members. . . . So then, I of myself serve the law of God with my mind, but with my flesh I serve the law of sin.
>
> ROMANS 7:15-19; 21-23; 25

Our own daily experience, if we are honest with ourselves, convinces us that by nature we are more tempted to do evil than good. Man is inclined to disobey God rather than to obey him. Good and kind and noble acts represent a positive triumph. Man is selfish and spiteful, envious of the good or indifferent to the pain of others without making the slightest effort to be that way.

Where there is no sin, there is no need for salvation. By repudiating the sinfulness of humanity, communism makes a mockery out of the Cross that stands at the center of Christian faith. According to communism there was no reason for Christ to come to earth and no need at all for him to suffer and die and rise again to save a lost world. The Communists themselves can save the world without him. They claim that when they have liquidated all opposition they will by their own technology, directed as they see fit, bring in the endless age of harmony and universal well-being right here on this planet, without the help of anyone or anything. Their one concern is to carry out faithfully the party's directions. If they do that, no wrongdoing can be charged against them.

Communism, which is blind to the reality of God and the human soul, disregards the Christian view of the reality of sin.

Without Reservation

Jesus Christ demonstrated complete dedication of life to one supreme task. He leaves no doubt that anyone who would follow him must do the same:

> . . . If any man would come after me, let him deny himself and take up his cross and follow me. For whoever would save his life will lose it, and whoever loses his life for my sake will find it.
>
> MATTHEW 16:24-25

The life and writings of Paul throb with this same spirit. He, too, lived for one consuming purpose. He had no ambition save that of knowing and proclaiming Jesus Christ. His own description of his sacrifice for the cause sounds more like the struggle of a modern revolutionary than the life of a nominal church member.

> Five times I have received at the hands of the Jews forty lashes less one. Three times I have been beaten with rods; once I was stoned. Three times I have been shipwrecked; a night and a day I have been adrift at sea; on frequent journeys, in danger from rivers, danger from robbers, danger from my own people, danger from Gentiles . . . in toil and hardship, through many a sleepless night, in hunger and thirst, often without food, in cold and exposure.
>
> 2 CORINTHIANS 11:24-27

The contagion of the spirit of this great first century Christian enabled the members of the early church to survive the opposition of their contemporaries in the Roman Empire. Twentieth-century Christians are called to enter into as sacrificial a struggle with foes of their faith. They are members of the Body of Christ and instruments in his hands to do his will in the world.

| Chapter 6 | The Christian's Responsibility |

Today Christians all over the world are united in an ecumenical fellowship and in varied ministries to human need. Members of all churches are accepting new responsibilities for sacrificial service in Christ's name.

National autonomous churches are growing out of nineteenth-century missionary endeavor, and overseas Christians are carrying on new work as trained national Christians become ministers and teachers. The churches have produced new agencies and developed new techniques for effective cooperation. Vast enterprises are afoot for relief and rehabilitation in war-torn and underdeveloped countries. Literacy campaigns have produced an effective attack on conditions in isolated villages. Radio, television, motion pictures, and mass-produced literature carry the Christian gospel into ancient villages and into crowded new cities, opening the way for the application of this gospel with spiritual power to the solution of pressing human problems.

World Evangelism

Christians today are engaged in an unprecedented campaign of world evangelism and ministries reaching out to intellectuals, industrial workers, masses of rural folk, and ever-growing new city populations in all parts of the world. Some Christians make direct personal contacts, the basic element in all evangelism, but many more are also utilizing all the modern means of mass communication to present the Christian gospel.

The Christian approach to men must be a total approach of

this kind, combining with Christian preaching and teaching and service all other means available to present the Christian truth with its application to particular situations in which men and women find themselves. With the means that are at the disposal of Christian churches today and with churches now established in every part of the world, Christians are in a position to present the message of Christ as never before in history.

Study and Action

Study and action are marks of the program of modern Christians. In Europe and Asia intellectuals and laborers are forming discussion and action groups, seeking with church groups answers to difficult questions.

This renewed Christian vigor is seen as the action of God in history. The Holy Spirit is at work, and urgency rests upon every believer to bear a social witness.

The Foundation for Social Witness

The Christian as a person is both a member of a religious body, the church, and a citizen of the state. He witnesses that Christ died for the redemption of man and lives today to over-rule men and nations. He proclaims that history finds its meaning and receives its final judgment in God through Christ. Such witness and proclamation in home, church, school, and community, in business and politics combats every form of "unfaith" when it reaches man at the level of his daily life.

Separated from God, man finds life meaningless enslavement to little goals and superficial plans. When God is replaced by idolatry of things and tyranny to things, the impersonal rule of economic and social forces gains control of the whole of life. The church in the Middle Ages had an elaborate pattern to show the way society should be organized. When medieval revolutionaries attacked the evils of their time, it was to the teachings of Christianity that they appealed.

With the beginning of more modern times, the peasant revolt seized its ideology from Christian belief. A century later revolution began in England led by the ardently religious Puritans. The most radical groups of that time were those Christian extremists called the "Levellers" and the "Diggers." Much of the drive for justice in social thinking that dominated Marx in the middle of the nineteenth century can be traced back to those groups in the time of Cromwell. The abolition of slavery around the world was largely spearheaded by the Christian conscience.

This long history of Christian social concern has its roots back in the earliest Christian beliefs and Scriptures. The Bible lays the main foundation stones for Christian action in society. The Christian view of creation is that the world is the handiwork of God as revealed in the first chapters of Genesis. The truth that God made all men of one blood and that man is his brother's keeper are biblical concepts.

The Old Testament prophets taught that God demands justice in all human relationships and that God so ordered the world that those who exploit and oppress their fellow men must suffer his judgment. These prophets spoke out boldly against all injustice and warned the people of impending doom. To those who were concerned about getting rich and in so doing sold "the righteous for silver, and the needy for a pair of shoes" (Amos 2:6), Amos announced the coming day of the Lord, which shall be "darkness, and not light" (Amos 5:20), for God will destroy all oppressors.

God still speaks through his prophet, telling his people that he cannot accept the worship of men who do not concern themselves first of all with justice:

> I hate, I despise, your feasts,
>> and I will take no delight in your solemn
>>> assemblies. . . .
> Take away from me the noise of your songs;
>> to the melody of your harps I will not
>>> listen.
> But let justice roll down like waters,
>> and righteousness like an ever-flowing
>>> stream.

Amos 5:21, 23-24

How Far Can the Church Go?

The church has a clear directive for action in community and national life. The chief problem it faces is how to find effective ways to go about this action.

The church is not a political party; it is not organized to exercise economic power. Therefore it cannot order that wrongs be righted nor change the economic and political system by its decree. What is more, the church should not do such things. No economic or political system comes up to Christian standards. No perfect system can be expected in the world as it is. Therefore the church dare not identify the Christian faith with any particular program.

Because this is true, Christians who are faced with the challenge of communism sometimes feel frustrated. "Communism has a clear-cut political and economic program," they say. "How can we meet it unless we also have specific plans?" Here Christians only show their lack of understanding of the strength of Christianity, for Christians can glory in their freedom from a concise, predetermined program rather than be embarrassed by the lack of one. This freedom means that people of many different political allegiances and economic philosophies can be part of the church and that the church can unite men of all times and all countries in a way that communism can never do. Further, it means that Christianity can survive the rise and fall of economic and political systems, which philosophies that are bound to a particular system have seldom been able to do.

Christians lived under the mighty imperial power of Rome with its countless hordes of slaves. In feudal days both the nobles and the serfs were Christians. In modern times Christians live under absolute monarchy, limited monarchy, democracy, and dictatorship. All of these systems have not been equally favorable to Christianity. Some have certainly been better and more amenable to Christian influence than others. Yet the basic fact remains, no system can separate man against his will from the love of Christ.

In this matter of faith, no man and no system has final power over man. Therefore Christians are fundamentally free; their freedom is given by God and it can neither be granted nor taken away by any man. The lack of a comprehensive, ironclad political program is only the negative aspect of this Christian freedom. It may be a short-term disadvantage in meeting powerful political movements, but in the long run such flexibility and openness is of tremendous advantage.

Seeing all this, Christians are thrown back again to the question: How then can the church carry out its social responsibilities? If it must include in its fellowship men of many different political and economic camps, if it cannot adopt any social system as its own, then is it not forced to keep quiet and do little or nothing about social problems? Not at all! There are at least three very important things that the church does:

1. The church holds up the ideal standard of Christ and the Christian conscience as the best measure of all social systems.

2. The church educates its members on the problems and needs of society as seen from the vantage point of the Christian conscience. It encourages individual and group action by responsible Christian citizens along social, economic, and political lines.

3. The church provides a center of love and strength for its members as they seek to advance the cause of Christ in their own community and other places. Each of these areas of action enfolds a great variety of possibilities.

Christian Conscience

Holding up the standards of Christ for social life is the most basic function of the church in this field. A standard or goal is the first necessity of social action. Without it as a point of reference, Christians cannot see where they are or in what direction they should move. Holding up such standards need not and must not be confined to the reiterating of platitudes with which everyone agrees. There is a middle ground between generalities on the one hand and specific political programs on the other. The church can say that the opportunity for all men to work is a standard that the economic system must meet. This is more specific than a general principle, such as "Love one another," yet it does not define particular legislative bills on unemployment insurance or control of the business cycle as being specifically Christian.

The church can also point out specific ills in society that call for a cure. Many pronouncements by churches are condemnations of specific evils that call for redress. A fine example of an heroic pronouncement against social evils came from the church in Norway at the time of the Hitler occupation. When the church saw law and justice being threatened and when the judges of the supreme court had to resign, the church spoke out boldly condemning acts of the government that were contrary to the Christian conscience. In one of their first statements, the Bishops

[75]

of Norway proclaimed, "Christians confess Jesus Christ as their Lord, totally and without reserve. The duty to be obedient to him stands above everything else." Bishop Berggrav declared, "Government stands under the law of God. The church must not be the government, but it must proclaim the law of God to the government." This view is that the church and the state have but one Lord and King: Jesus Christ. Therefore the church must be the conscience of the state, telling it when it violates the laws of God.

The function of the church to raise Christian standards grows out of its nature as a free, voluntary community within society. It is a channel of divine truth and love even in nations where such virtues are officially distorted. In any situation the church can maintain contact between the power of God and sinful humanity. It witnesses to his presence and concern though all others may deny his existence. It defies the world through the reliance upon God's power that Jesus evidenced when he said:

> "I will no longer talk much with you, for the ruler of this world is coming. He has no power over me; but I do as the Father has commanded me, so that the world may know that I love the Father. . . . "
>
> JOHN 14:30-31

Social Education and Action

A comparative study of communism and Christianity is only the beginning of the type of social education that is needed on the part of the church. Christians should be just as well acquainted with the strong and weak points of other economic and social systems. They need to understand how the profit motive, free competition, and government regulation work ideally. They should be able to express some Christian judgment on the so-called "capitalist" theory that the greatest good will be served best by intelligent, responsible self-interest and by present-day democratic enterprise's modifications of capitalism. They should understand why monopolies develop and learn what steps have been taken to curb them and with what success.

Christians need to appreciate the importance of decentralization in economic life and the establishment of independent centers of economic initiative in this day of large corporations and various state economic systems. They should sense what the ad-

vancement of democratic enterprise has meant to much exploited
nations in Asia, Africa, and Latin America. They should be able
to state how far the charge that "capitalism produces imperialism" is true and to compare the types of "imperialism" and "colonialism" found in the world today. They should know both the
benefits and the dangers of widespread social planning.

The need is for Christians who as conscientious citizens will
study social situations honestly, form intelligent opinions, and
take positive action where such action will meet human needs.
Partisans who have something to gain or lose personally through
their study usually form violently one-sided opinions.

More churchmen must come to realize that all people, including themselves, have much to gain or lose in the answers society
gives to economic, social, and political questions. When Christians have honestly studied these questions and tried to bring
opposing groups together in their studies, the results in terms of
general agreement have often far exceeded expectations. When
labor and management have met, not as proponents of their
own particular ideas but as Christians joined to seek and know
the will of God, they have found they agree basically on a wide
range of subjects.

Positive Christian Witness

After study comes action. The church can seldom go into the
field of direct political and economic action, but individual Christians and groups are free to go forward as they are led by God,
illuminated by the studies they have made.

An example of how study leads to action comes from the rural
and coastal area of Nova Scotia. A Christian college was located
there among depressed and impoverished fishermen, and one
of its professors began going among the common people. He did
not offer them a blueprint for action but he got them interested
in studying the situation. He gathered men about him and read
to them. He left pamphlets and books, brought in speakers, and
held public meetings. Gradually the people awoke to the realiza-
tion that something could be done about their condition. They
saw that education was the main thing they needed and suggested that the college organize study groups.

A program known as the Antigonish movement developed in
the course of years of experimenting. A recent estimate calls it a

"blending of adult education, Christian ethics, and a program of social justice directed through a university extension department."[1] It is basically an educational approach to social progress and not simply an economic movement.

The college formed study groups, led by local leaders who had been discovered in the public meetings. The courses in reading, economics, sociology, cooperative methods and philosophies, public speaking, and recent history had to be close to the problems of the people. The effort was made to clarify the problems. College experts were at hand ready to help when the people decided what they wanted to do.

Out of these study groups came the idea of a cooperative canning factory. With technical help provided by the college, the idea rapidly became a reality. The venture finally succeeded and to a large extent made the fishermen independent of the merchants on whom they had depended for the sale of their products.

After the cooperative factory came a credit union that freed people from debt slavery. Then came other producers'–consumers' cooperatives. Gradually the whole standard of living in the area changed. A new independence and self-respect developed among the people. Not only their material condition but also their psychological and spiritual condition was transformed by the action they had taken.

The Antigonish Movement never regarded cooperatives as ends in themselves. "They were promoted both as instruments of education and as a means to a better social order."[2] Similarly, the Antigonish Movement is not cited here as an argument for or against any form of social or economic organization. It is used to show that Christians as individuals and groups are free to study and to act as they are led by God.

Another example of effective Christian action is found in Denmark, where many years ago church leaders established credit unions, cooperative stores, and the renowned folk schools that have done so much to make Denmark a progressive, democratic, and self-reliant nation. Under Christian leadership the folk schools and cooperatives have provided a democratic method of community development. The schools are an active feature of life in other Scandinavian countries.

The teaching in these schools was largely in cultural subjects with much group singing and manual work to develop a sense of community in all of life. Out of these schools have come the leaders in the transformation of rural life in those lands. They have created a responsible, alert, and enlightened citizenry, active in political and economic affairs.

Many people have wondered why it is that the labor movement in Great Britain has not developed along the lines of revolutionary action and extremism that have characterized much of labor's growth in other chief countries of Europe. British labor has consistently followed a more constructive and, in the long run, apparently successful policy. The reason may well lie in the vigorous Christian leadership given to that movement by dedicated laymen of the Methodist and some of the other free churches for the past century and a half. Many a time it happened that the ruling committee of the labor union and the responsible body of the church were made up of the same men. While fulfilling their obligations in the life of the church these men naturally turned to the consideration of their obligations in the community.

At times such social action on a community or national scale is not enough. There are countries where no amount of constructive social thinking and planning will work unless international trade can be carried on in such a way as to open up economic opportunities. In these cases Christian social responsibility encompasses the world and calls for some unifying fellowship and some common approach. Awakened Christians in one land need to aid and support those in other lands.

Members of the Christian church, even in nations under Communist control, can depend upon the power and providence of God, seeking spiritual renewal that the continued existence of the church may in itself be an effective witness to freedom in Christ. Renewal in the Christian community breaks forth at times with astonishing vigor, and from unlikely places and people. A small group of students a century and a half ago met for a prayer meeting under a haystack and released immense missionary fervor that led to world-wide missionary movement. Dwight L. Moody, a converted shoe salesman, was the instrument of a mighty revival movement. A few laymen launched the world-wide organization of the Young Men's Christian Association. From the efforts of another layman, Dr. R. von Thadden-

Trieglaff, has sprung forth in divided Germany the Evangelica' Kirchentag, or Church Assembly, which displays a new sense of world-wide responsibility and brotherhood.

Both Christians directly under Communist authority and Christians who feel the long range threat of communism must learn how to resist ominous pressure with love. Without resorting to war, Christians seek ways to restrain Communist aggression and to preserve the God-given freedom of every citizen to participate in the building of a just state. To change society in accord with the will of God and to witness to trust in him as it is revealed in any situation requires much wisdom and patience.

Christian action is taking place through many ministries performed with non-Christians in face-to-face, person-to-person relationships. Around the world Christians are ministering across national and racial lines, in group-to-group exchanges. The power, riches, and techniques now entrusted to men must be shared, not to exert pressure or to express judgment or to gain a favorable vote but to bring men into a closer relationship with God. True ministry cannot be through money alone or through might but in the spirit of Jesus who said, "I am the way, and the truth, and the life; no one comes to the Father but by me." The ministry of reconciliation has at least three goals: that all may be one in Christ; that life in today's world may be meaningful; that harmony in society may be sought and enjoyed.

Responsible Living

Responsible living is a form of Christian action expected of every believer. This responsibility is assumed in the light of knowledge of God and the nature of man. Reminding themselves very often of the biblical basis for all their social witness, Christians can take a stand and act on economic questions, not because of any success they are sure to achieve but because they know God's love for the world and for every individual in that world and must express what that love means in concrete terms. Informed, concerned, committed Christians feel a compulsion to make their witness in deed as well as in word.

It is not required of a Christian that he be successful in all he does. It is only required of him that he be faithful. The issue is in the hands of God. Christians can always witness in some way, running "with perseverance the race that is set before

[them], looking to Jesus the pioneer and perfecter of [their] faith" (Hebrews 12:1-2). As Christians throughout the world respond to Christ's imperative "Go . . . teach," they will seize the initiative to effect social change with justice.

Men can do little to help build a more Christian world until their own hearts are changed, but men whose lives have been transformed turn naturally to the consideration of their obligations in the life of their community.

The Church, a Center of Love and Power

Any group of laymen or any minister can take the first step by bringing together a small fellowship group of concerned men and women to seek together to know God's will for their church with a willingness to obey that will as it is revealed to them.

The early Christian church was such a fellowship of small groups who believed in Christ. They were motivated by the all-consuming passion to preach Christ and serve him as their Lord. They met together, prayed together, shared their joys and sorrows, and helped one another when in need. They were the powerhouse of the church of the first century.

New life comes into the church today whenever groups of men and women and young people meet together regularly for worship, study, and action. Individuals who are beginning to realize what is demanded of them as Christians in this time and who are aware of their own inadequacy in the face of that demand can strengthen and support one another through fellowship in prayer, Bible study, and reflection on ways by which the Word can be made real in a world such as ours. They can make an effective beginning by working out disciplines for their own daily lives and developing a program of action to be carried out through their church.

The combination of worship, study, and action is essential. Groups that hold these three elements in a vigorous and vital relationship meet constructively the challenge social situations pose, a challenge far too great for any individual to attempt to meet alone. Ever since Pentecost, the power of the church as the Body of Christ has been experienced primarily in a fellowship through which Christians with passionate devotion to Christ have opened their hearts to God. Together across national and racial and class lines they have faced world dangers and needs.

[81]

How Can This Be Accomplished?

Certainly strong emphasis on the Christian's responsibility to serve should be in the curriculum and program of every youth and adult organization in the church, and in preparation for church membership. Every local church should have a Committee on Social Education and Action that will provide an opportunity for open discussion of important issues and keep church members informed on specific ways in which they can express their sense of responsibility in action.

Every Christian should be called to become an active participant in some phase of social education and action through which he can serve his fellow man. Such service includes social work, literacy projects, work among children and youth, rural and urban projects. It embraces support of the United Nations and working for racial justice through local church and interchurch programs. And it should not stop there. The Christian's action, to have relevance and to be effective, needs to be carried on within other institutions that determine the life of man today. Important in this connection are the labor movements, farmers' organizations, business, and politics. It is here that the basic decisions affecting men are being made. The Christian cannot flee this responsibility because it is difficult. Rather he should seek it as the will of God for his life and work at it passionately.

A New Sense of Christian Vocation

God calls men to serve him not only in his Church but also in society. When Christians in every area of life see their work as an opportunity that God has given to them to serve him and their neighbor, a tremendous power for good will be let loose that can have a great influence in transforming society.

This happened in the Wesleyan revival in England. William Wilberforce, one of Wesley's converts, felt the call of God to free the Negro slaves and he gave his life to that work. The day he died the English Parliament abolished slavery. Another convert gave his life and wealth to prison reform, another to care for orphaned children, another to serve the abandoned industrial workers. Each gave himself to his task in response to the call of God.

Every follower of Christ has a Christian vocation, a call from

God to meet some human need. Young people are called to serve God in the labor movement, in politics, in a crusade for better race relations. The world needs doctors, nurses, teachers, farmers, industrial workers, and businessmen who see in their work the opportunity God has given them to serve him. As Christians accept such calls and fulfill them with vigor and devotion, Communists will be confronted with men and women who have a passion to match their own, men and women supremely concerned about human need and struggling daily for social justice. Such Christians will offer a genuine new hope for the future of the world.

Self-Examination

When the full light of God's revelation in Jesus Christ shines on the teaching of communism, its errors stand glaringly revealed. But a candid examination of society around the world reveals to an alarming degree that many people who are not Communists believe and practice the same things that Communists do. The reason is simple: Marx and communism are by-products of the growth and worship of industry and science, the major forces that tend to shape our contemporary world—the entire world, not just some isolated sphere of Communist influence. The Communists, however, have put their ideas together into a coherent plan of thought and action. Three points must be honestly faced.

1. Millions of people today worship science and deny God's Providence. They are not Communists, but they worship science, deny God's Providence, ignore the reality of the human soul, and give little or no thought to moral sin. They have not accepted Marxian communism, but they live by some or all of its principles. For all practical purposes their lives are quite empty of God. Their real trust is in themselves, in their own cleverness and resourcefulness. In fact an economic system of free enterprise, such as predominates in the West, does a lot to encourage that sort of attitude.

2. Millions of people fail to regard all mankind as sons of God. They may feel that they value the human individual much more than Communists do but may not do so for the Christian reason or in the Christian way. They do not genuinely regard all men as created by God with equal value in his eyes. If they

did, some of the statements in our democratic constitutions would be more than ideals, and there would be a real understanding that economic exploitation and bitter social injustice afford communism a fertile breeding ground.

3. Millions of people shut their eyes to the reality of sin. They seem to feel that, in view of the marvelous strides of modern technology toward controlling disease, banishing hunger, and providing a heretofore undreamed-of living standard, hope can be promised the world's sufferers that the kingdom of heaven or something like it can readily be achieved on earth. "After all," they say, "people are not really bad. Let's look on the bright side and things will get better." In so saying, they shut their their eyes to the reality of sin just as truly as Communists do.

How Do You Read?

When an educated inquirer once asked Jesus what the great commandment was, Jesus responded by asking him what was written in the law of God. "How do you read?" he inquired. How do you read today the meaning of Christianity and the meaning of communism for yourself?

The great appeal of communism to people of high ideals is that it proposes a prompt and vigorous remedy for some of the worst evils in modern society. Christians in many countries have felt the force of that appeal. They have asked themselves, "Can this movement be evil when its followers fight against social evils? Should not Christians, while keeping their eyes open, co-operate with communism, at least to a limited degree, as long as it continues to work toward really Christian objectives?"

You must answer such questions for yourself. But remember other Christians who have been brought to realize that any system, whatever its slogans or outward program, that denies God and the dignity and worth of all his children leads the Christian only into a dead-end street. At length a point is reached beyond which there is no way but a renunciation: either faith in communism or faith in Christ must go.

Credits

CHAPTER 1

1. *I Chose Freedom,* by Victor Kravchenko. New York, Charles Scribner's Sons, 1946.
2. *The Christian Science Monitor,* July 5, 1960, p. 9.
3. *The New York Times,* August 19, 1961, p. 2.
4. *The God That Failed,* Richard Crossman, Editor. New York, Harper and Brothers, 1950.

CHAPTER 2

1. *State and Revolution,* by N. Lenin, p. 74.
2. *The New York Times,* August 1, 1961, Section L, p. 18.
3. *Ibid.,* p. 10.

CHAPTER 3

1. *The New York Times,* August 1, 1961, Section L, p. 13.
2. *The New York Times,* October 18, 1961, p. 16.
3. *The Church in Communist China,* by Francis Price Jones. New York, Friendship Press, 1961, pp. 45, 46.
4. *China Consultation, 1958,* New York, Far Eastern Office, Division of Foreign Missions, National Council of Churches of Christ in the U.S.A., pp. 7-8, 11.
5. *The New York Times,* October 25, 1961.
6. Quoted in *Christianity Today,* October 27, 1961.

CHAPTER 4

1. *Religion,* by N. Lenin, p. 7.
2. Quoted in *A Christian's Handbook on Communism,* New York, Committee on World Literacy and Christian Literature, 1952. Source unknown.
3. Quoted in *A Primer on Communism,* by George W. Cronyn. New York, E. P. Dutton & Co., Inc., 1961, p. 80.
4. Quoted from Moscow Radio Broadcast, March 27, 1958, in *Soviet World Outlook, A Handbook of Communist Statements.* Washington, Department of State, 1959, p. 78.
5. *The New York Times,* October 16, 1961.

CHAPTER 5

1. *Stalin, A Political Biography,* by Isaac Deutscher. New York and London, Oxford University Press, 1948.

CHAPTER 6

1. Quoted from *Information Service,* Vol. XL, No. 21, Part 1. New York, Bureau of Research and Survey, National Council of Churches, 1961.
2. *Ibid.*

11 - 401